C000254184

sampler

CAROLINE VINCENT

workbook

MOTIFS & PATTERNS

First published in Great Britain 2010
A&C Black Publishers Ltd.,
36 Soho Square W1D 3QY
www.acblack.com

Copyright © 2010 Caroline Vincent

ISBN: 978-1-4081-1015-7

All rights reserved. No part of this publication may be reproduced in any form or by any means – graphic, electronic or mechanical, including photocopying, recording, taping or information storage and retrieval systems – without the prior permission in writing from the publishers.

Caroline Vincent has asserted her right under the Copyright, Design and Patents Act, 1988, to be identified as the author of this work.

A CIP catalogue record for this book is available from the British Library.

Printed and Bound in China by C&C Offset Printing Co., Ltd.

contents

ACKNOWLEDGEMENTS.

My grateful thanks to the Curators of the following museums for their help and assistance. City of Bristol Museum and Art Gallery, Dorset County Museum, Embroiderers' Guild Hampton Court Palace, Fitzwilliam Museum, Glasgow Museum, Gloucester Folk Museum, National Trust Montacute House, Royal Pavillion and Museums Brighton and Hove, Victoria and Albert Museum, Witney Antiques.
I would also like to thank Paul Jenkins for the photography, Madeira UK Ltd for supplying threads, Colin Fulford of Fulford Software Solutions and Rosa Farr, Hollie Saunders and Edwin Wood for allowing me to use details from commissioned samplers.

CHAPTER ONE
introduction

The art of embroidery has provided a form of individual and creative expression for generations of needleworkers, and the immediacy of the simple tools and techniques, gives this ancient craft its universal appeal. The definition of the word embroider, is to decorate, ornament and visually enhance, but throughout the history of textiles it has also been used as a means of communication, with various images and symbols having the ability to convey a meaningful message, long before the written word. The Bayeux Tapestry is a wonderful example of a story narrated in picture form, and this amazing piece of needlework displays many characteristics of later samplers, with the main pictorial composition placed between two narrow borders, together with a strong theme of pattern, created by the use of repeat motifs, and also the inclusion of descriptive text. A number of the motifs used in early samplers held particular symbolic and religious meanings, and although many of these were to gradually become less significant, the figurative image has always created its own story and encouraged imaginative interpretation. The charm of the pictorial sampler lies in the fantasy world it conjures up, where images can exist in the same space regardless of relative proportion and scale, and traditional and contemporary themes are able to sit comfortably together in the same composition. The unsophisticated style and pleasing nature of the work, makes this appealing and attractive form of embroidery an activity that can be enjoyed by anyone, regardless of age or previous experience.

The great tradition of English embroidery was established during the Middle Ages, when the production of richly decorated ecclesiastical furnishings developed into a thriving industry, that was eventually exported all over the continent. The magnificent embroideries were listed in church inventories alongside the reference Opus Anglicanum, which meant English work, and this term came to be regarded as the trademark for a standard of excellent workmanship. The beautiful copes and alter cloths made from the finest silks and velvets, were covered with precious metal threads, pearls, jewels and beaten gold, and the best artists were commissioned to make the designs, as embroidery at that time was considered a leading art form, alongside painting and sculpture. During this period both men and women were employed in the production of these intricate masterpieces and the growing demand for the embroideries, meant that the regular source of supply through the convents and monasteries was overwhelmed with the quantity of orders, and to ease the situation small rural workshops were formed and gradually developed into guilds. Larger establishments were finally centred in London and run as commercial businesses by professional embroiderers and merchants, who were able to charge extortionate prices for their exquisite craftsmanship.

This overwhelming interest and passion for ornament and decoration gradually extended to articles of clothing and domestic furnishings, and during the late 14th century a detailed record for a country estate lists a number of large four poster beds, all with luxurious hangings and one in particular covered with 'silver owls and fluers de lys'. By the mid-16th century the indulgent lifestyle of the titled nobility, was to reach even more extravagant proportions, when the sum of fourteen thousand pounds was paid for a 'white satin hanging decorated with silver and pearls'. Besides their commissioned work from the church, nuns were required to oversee any mending and alterations, but such was the demand for embroidered accessories, such as purses, bags and belts, that many convents would supplement their meagre income by taking in fine needlework for ladies. However, this state of prosperity was not to last, and the onset of the War with France and the decimating effect of the Black Death, which affected almost half the convents in England, meant that not only was a skilled and reliable workforce greatly reduced, but that a source of education and apprenticeship for many young girls was no longer available.

During the 16th century, English embroidery began a further period of decline and the disbanding of the craft guilds together with the Dissolution of the Monasteries meant that many of the priceless embroideries, including copes and alter cloths were plundered and dismantled for their gold content and precious stones. Other items were cut into pieces and sold off, to be used as furnishings in stately homes and who knows how many other lesser pieces of embroidery were lost in the fires and destruction that ravaged the country. However, other changes were gradually taking place and as a new class of wealthy merchants and gentlemen began to acquire substantial landed properties, the interest in decorating and furnishing their domestic environments, continued to grow. The competition and rivalry between families, to outdo each other and create the most comfortable and fashionable of establishments, created a whole new opportunity for women to direct the interior design of their own homes, and so began the rise of the amateur embroiderer. Besides employing journeyman craftsmen to offer advice on the designs, and provide some technical expertise whilst overseeing the projects, everyone eligible in the household, would be included in this flurry of activity to decorate bed-curtains, valances, table carpets, cushions and array of smaller items such as book-covers, shoes, gloves and nightcaps. The ownership of fine textiles and embroideries was equated with wealth and status, and there are many accounts of the prolific array of needlework, that was instigated by the inspirational and ambitious personality, 'Bess of Hardwick Hall'.

For the first half of the 16th century, a period of social unrest existed for several decades and young girls, who might previously have been sent to board in a convent, now had the opportunity to join the women of the household in learning their needlework skills, whist also perhaps have

additional instruction from a private tutor. It was not until the stability of the Elizabethan era, when the Arts and Literature were able to once again flourish, that attitudes towards the education of young girls began to advance. A number of convents were re-opened, but more significantly, private schools were soon established to teach a range of gentile accomplishments, including fine embroidery. The incredible amount of samplers that have survived from the Stuart period, which are usually described as spot or band samplers, provide a wonderful reference and insight into the exacting standards of work expected from girls aged as young as eight years. The perfectly stitched rows of patterns that appear to have been completed for the sole purpose of practising needlework skills and stitch techniques, often give the impression that they were produced under the strict supervision of a teacher and the contrast between these very formal embroideries and the haphazard and disorganised placement of motifs in many of the spot samplers, suggests that perhaps they were pieces made in the less disciplined environment of the family home, and inspired by the work directed towards domestic furnishings. A number of band samplers include similar patterns and motifs, and the distinctive styles and arrangement of the designs, implies that they may have originated from the same source, perhaps through circulating patterns or a particular school setting.

The earliest group of samplers to be attributed to a particular teacher were worked under the tuition of Judith Hayle, who ran a small school from her home in Ipswich. The first recorded sampler dates from the last decade of the 17th century, and all the samplers are marked with her initials, with some referring to her directly as the 'mistris or dame'. The overall, individual style of some of the later pieces is quite recognisable, and Judith was later joined by her daughter, who continued to run the school after her death. With an increasing concern for the need to provide an elementary education for the less advantaged, a number of Charity schools were formed which taught plain needlework and darning skills, in order to prepare young girls for a life in service, where they would be required to mend and initial the laundry. Towards the end of the 18th century the Ackworth School was founded in York, which was to offer a standard education for children of Quaker families regardless of their social position. The most specific and easily identifiable style of these very detailed and finely stitched embroideries, included a series of patterns based on geometric forms, that were designed to encourage the understanding of basic mathematical problems. A further significant group of samplers, that were to represent a particular institution, were all produced by the children attending the Bristol Orphanages, during the middle part of the 19th century. The carefully composed embroideries, consisting of rows of alphabets, verse and a range of narrow border designs, were invariably worked in plain red and always signed and dated, and for many young girls might have provided a welcome and satisfying diversion from the harsh realities of daily life.

The style and content of the sampler began to change significantly in the 18th century, with the emphasis on practising techniques being replaced by pictorial compositions, which were increasingly influenced by the patterns and motifs illustrated in Dutch and German pattern books. The sampler embroidery was now an established part of the school curriculum and the suitability of the simple cross-stitch technique for not only interpreting the angular forms of the alphabets, numerals and verses that featured in almost every sampler, but also the simplicity of the uniform stitch made it a most efficient and effective solution for the teacher supervising a large class. Eventually, the enthusiasm for the sampler gradually began to wane, and as the very fine linens and muslins, which had dictated the meticulous needlework of previous generations, were replaced with coarser fabrics, the variation and complexity of the compositions also began to decline. By the middle of the 19th century a new form of needlework picture, generally known as Berlin woolwork, was to finally bring about the demise of the traditional sampler, as the brightly coloured embroideries became instantly popular with a public looking for a new and exciting contemporary style.

The religious and political turmoil that raged through England and Europe during the 17th century resulted in many persecuted communities fleeing their homelands and trusting in the safety of a new life in America. Thousands of English, Dutch and German families were to settle in areas around New England and Pennsylvania, bringing with them not only the few treasured possessions that included various pieces of needlework, but also a whole wealth of traditional culture and artistic creative skills. With very few materials available to hand, women were required use all their talents and resourcefulness, as they re-created a comfortable and decorative environment in the home. Crewelwork hangings and coverlets, patchwork bedspreads, and needlework pictures were tirelessly produced by every family, and so began the great tradition of American textiles. Initially the patterns and motifs on many of the early embroideries were directly influenced by the more formal compositions of previous works, but gradually a freer and more abandoned approach to the subject, was to eventually develop into the highly individual and expressive style, that is the hallmark of the American sampler. By the beginning of the 18th century, a number of schools and academies were being established in rapid succession, and many were run specifically by young mistresses who had trained in England. The competition to attract students was fierce, and several schools soon developed a particular style and method of working that was instantly recognisable as a standard of creative achievement. Pupils were able to stay at a school until their late teens, but the majority of the inscriptions, on these highly accomplished pictorial samplers, indicate that the girls were generally aged between eight and thirteen years, although much younger children could be enrolled at a school, and initially taught basic sewing skills in order to complete a plain marking sampler, before embarking on a more ambitious project. An examination at the end of each year would select the most notable pieces for an exhibition, to be attended by proud parents and local dignitaries, before the framed embroideries were taken home to be further admired.

The endless diversity and visual appeal of the American sampler, in many ways reflects the artistic aspirations and personal commitment of the talented young schoolmistresses, who encouraged an imaginative and individual approach to the subject. A number of schools were renowned for their distinctive designs and quality of needlework, and amongst some of the most notable examples are the wonderful embroideries from Miss Sarah

Stivour's School in Salem, Massachusetts, which depict colourful landscape scenes, with areas of grass and sky worked in very long diagonal stitches, using a type of crinkly silk that created a characteristic lustrous sheen. Another important group of samplers were worked at Mary Balch's Academy in Providence, Rhode Island, which included numerous examples of local architecture, together with small scenes depicting detailed figures, dressed in fashionable attire. Several lively compositions based on rural themes, including large lawns scattered with various animals, were produced in the Quaker schools of Burlington County, New Jersey, and also the magnificent and original style of the farm samplers, that are thought to have been inspired by Martha Barber, who ran a small school in Marblehead, Massachusetts. These are just a few examples, among many pieces of beautiful needlework that were produced in homes, village schools and academies throughout almost two centuries, and continued until the middle of the 19th century when the long tradition of sampler-making finally suffered the same fate as the English sampler. As an embroiderer myself, I feel very fortunate that so many international museums and galleries, together with individual collectors and benefactors, have carefully preserved these enchanting pieces of needlework, in order that future generations can continue to appreciate this unique artform, that has left a legacy of inspirational and innovative ideas for which I am much indebted.

PLANNING A DESIGN

Many of the patterns and motifs that feature on the following pages have been inspired by traditional designs, which I have adapted, altered and re-interpreted in my own style. The colours chosen to illustrate the charted designs, are only possible suggestions and reflect the range of colours I use in my own embroideries, which are achieved through mixing and blending different shades and tones of the coloured threads. Various colours may need to be changed according to the theme of your proposed design, and besides the many variations and permutations that can be made when combining two or three different coloured threads in the needle together, there are a huge range of colours readily available that will produce equivalent matches to many of the charted colours. The stitched examples that relate to the themed chapters, include a number of options for combining various lustre, metallic and rayon threads, to create contrasting textural surfaces and highlight particular areas of the design, and these ideas can be further developed and incorporated in alternative patterns. All the main charted designs are presented on the same sized graph, and therefore the motifs and patterns can be interchanged and re-arranged quite easily, to suit any personal requirements. The blank graph page at the end of the book also provides a further opportunity to plan various options, and create individual compositions.

MATERIALS AND EQUIPMENT
FABRICS

Evenweave fabrics are the ideal choice for working in cross-stitch, as the regular weave of the threads ensures that all your stitches will be uniform and equal in size. In the past linen was the most commonly used fabric, and although linen is still considered the ideal traditional material to use for a sampler, it can actually prove to be quite a difficult fabric to work with, as the closely textured quality of the cloth makes the definition of the holes in the weave slightly more taxing on the eyes, and therefore not always suitable for a large project, unless you already experienced with working on linen. Fortunately today, we have a whole variety of easier fabrics to work with, ranging from very fine weaves to the more open blockweave fabrics, such as Aida which is manufactured in such a way that the threads are arranged in blocks, so that the holes in the fabric are more easily visible.

When deciding on the type of fabric best suited to your requirements you will also need to think about the count of the fabric, which refers to the number of holes per inch or centimetre in the material. The higher the number of the count, the finer the quality of the weave, so a 32 count fabric will produce a very fine piece of needlework, whereas a 14 count Aida will produce a piece of work approximately twice the size. The most usual choice of fabric is a 28 count which is equivalent to a 16 count Aida, or a 25 count evenweave, which is compatible with a 14 count Aida.

FABRIC COLOURS

Besides making a decision about the type of fabric you wish to work on, the next most important consideration is the colour of the cloth, and nowadays there is a wonderful range of shades to choose from that can be matched to the style and content of your design. I personally prefer to work on a natural or ecru coloured fabric, as I feel that a more subtle background colour compliments and enhances the colours of the threads. A pure white fabric can appear very bright and stark in contrast with the coloured embroidery threads and has the tendency to compete with the colours, making even quite bright shades look rather dull, and it also has the added disadvantage of completely engulfing any colours from the white and cream ranges. The majority of traditional samplers were worked on natural coloured linens, and on occasions very dark coloured fabrics were deliberately chosen so that the composition could be entirely stitched in a range of very pale and pastel hues. Most of the evenweave fabrics have a good choice of muted and natural colours in their range of shades and there are some interesting examples in the Aida Rustico range.

I usually work on quite dark coloured fabrics and adapt my thread choices to match the shade of the cloth, and the particular effect I am trying to achieve with the patterns and motifs I am working from. I have decided to use a 28 count Brittney Light Mocha for all the stitched samples in the book, as it is a very neutral colour and although it might look quite dark to someone who has mainly used a white background, it will soon appear very light once you have begun stitching the motifs. The clearly defined weave of the cloth makes it very easy to see the holes when working, and the quality of the fabric makes it a pleasure to handle.

ZWEIGART FABRIC INFORMATION.

28 Count Brittney: cotton and rayon mix.
A good range of colours, and a clear regular weave which is easy to work.

28 Count Cashel: linen.
A wide range of natural and dyed colours, a more compact weave with a slightly slubby texture.

25 Count Lugana: cotton and rayon mix.
A good colour range, and an excellent fabric to work as the weave is very easy to see.

14 Count Aida: cotton or linen varieties.
These fabrics have been woven in the form of small blocks, and come in a range of sizes including 18,16,14, and 11. The Oatmeal coloured Rustico or the Natural Raw Linen, both make a more interesting fabric to work on and also tend to disguise the uniform appearance of the weave.

THREADS
EMBROIDERY COTTONS.
Stranded embroidery cottons are the most commonly used threads for cross-stitch, and the main thread is made up of six strands of mercerised cotton which gives the thread its distinctive sheen. The individual strands of a cut length need to be separated into single threads and then put back together in groups of two or three threads, depending on the type of fabric you are using. The huge range of colours produced by both DMC and Coats Craft provide an enormous choice of colour options that can be expanded further by mixing and blending different colours together, to create your own individual colour schemes.

METALLIC THREADS
The addition of metallic and lustre threads to a cross-stitch design provides many new possibilities for creating a more interesting and varied textural surface. The machine embroidery threads are usually the easiest to work with as they are both flexible and very fine, so that they can be combined with the stranded cotton skeins quite easily. The Madeira no.40, machine embroidery reels, include an excellent colour range with many lustre and metallic varieties. Contrasting and complementary surface textures can be made very easily by just combining and blending the different threads together.

HOOPS AND FRAMES
Whether or not to use a hoop or frame is really a matter of personal choice, and many embroiderers feel more comfortable simply holding the fabric in the hand, perhaps supported on a cushion. A hoop can be quite useful at the beginning of a project, particularly if you are starting with a large motif such as a building or tree, but once the embroidery is too big to fit inside the hoop, then it is best to discard it as the pressure of the rings on any stitches will crush

them, and spoil their appearance. The hoop is more suitable for smaller projects, whereas a frame is ideal for larger embroideries and there are many different options available in plastics or wood, including Flexi-hoops, Bar frames and Stretcher frames.

NEEDLES

Tapestry needles with a blunt end, and sharp pointed crewel needles with a long eye, are both suitable for sampler embroidery. Both types of needle are available in a range of graded sizes, with lower numbers for the thicker needles and higher numbers corresponding to the finer needles.

1 Crewel needles no. 5 and 6 are quite easy to thread and will comfortably hold three strands of thread. The higher nos.10 and 11 are particularly suitable for very fine work, such as petit-point, and will also pass through the holes in most small beads.
1 Tapestry needles in size 24 and 26 are suitable for most cross-stitch fabrics.
1 Bead needles are extremely fine and come in long and short lengths. They are quite difficult to thread and usually a needle-threader is required for rayon threads, however nylon invisible thread will pass through the eye quite easily.

BEADS: SEED BEADS, ROCAILLES, BUGLE BEADS

Using small beads to highlight certain areas of a floral pattern or decorative composition, is an ideal way of enriching a colour scheme and bringing added interest to a design. The wonderful range of colours and textures available, including beads with matt, glass, pearl, foil-lined and metallic finishes, provide endless possibilities for variation and creating different effects. The smallest beads sizes 15 and 11, are the most suitable for combining with cross-stitch patterns, and should be attached with rayon machine thread (Madeira no.40) or invisible nylon thread, making a double stitch through the bead to hold it in place.

GETTING STARTED.
SIZE OF FABRIC

Once you have made the decision about the type and colour of fabric to use, you will need to think about the size of the piece of material you will require in relation to your planned project. When you have completed your design and know the exact measurements, you should add an extra 8-11cm (3 - 4 inches) all the way round to allow for stretching and framing the embroidery. However, if you have not quite finalised your design then it is better to have a slightly larger piece of fabric, as you may decide to extend your composition or add a wider border pattern, and it is always better to have a bit of spare fabric, rather than be disappointed and unable to complete an alternative idea.

To calculate the scale of your design in relation to the different weights of the fabric, you will need to make a note of the number of the thread count, which corresponds to the number of stitches you will make every 2.5 cm or 1 inch. For instance a 28 count evenweave will equal 14 cross-stitches to the inch (2.5 cm) and if you then calculate the number of squares in the graph pattern and divide it by 14 you will have a fairly accurate guide to the size of you finished embroidery.

For example a graph of 168 squares x 140 squares = 12in x 10in (30.5cm x 25.5cm)

28 count evenweave = 14 cross stitches

168 squares ÷ 14 = 12

PREPARING THE FABRIC

First check that there are no flaws or marks on the fabric that will end up in a prominent position when the embroidery is finished, and then press out any creases in the fabric with a damp cloth and hot iron. Any stubborn fold lines, which are quite common on large pieces of fabric, may not disappear completely but I usually find that they are almost unnoticeable once the work is stretched.

The next step is to bind the edges of the fabric to stop it from fraying as you work, and you can either oversew the raw edges by hand or use a row of machine zigzag on a loose tension. On a small design that can be completed quite quickly it is not usually necessary, but on a large piece of fabric that will undergo much handling it will be essential, and I find one of the easiest and simplest methods is to bind the edges with masking tape and add a row of staples to keep the tape in place.

POSITIONING YOUR DESIGN ON THE FABRIC.

There are any number of places you can begin your embroidery and you do not have to start in the centre of the fabric. I usually start with one of the main motifs, such as a building or tree, and place in any surrounding motifs followed by the border patterns and finally adding delicate details such as eyes and back-stitch highlights at the very end. One easy method for beginning to sew is to lay your design on the fabric and pinpoint the exact place to start the first stitch, bearing in mind any difference in scale between the graph pattern and the count of the fabric. Alternatively you can mark out the centre of the fabric with tacking stitches or work a row of even running stitches close to the edge, across the top of the fabric, and then another row down the side of the fabric. On a larger, embroidery I will often work further rows of running stitch at various intervals across the centre of the fabric and I find this very useful for positioning motifs, when I am not working from a set design.

MAKING THE FIRST STITCH

When beginning an area of cross-stitch it is important to make sure that the first stitch is secured carefully and once an area of embroidery is laid in place, any new colours can be added by simply running the threads through the back of the embroidery and working a small back-stitch to hold the thread secure. However, a different technique is needed when starting on a bare piece of fabric, and there are various methods that can be used to secure the first stitches.

1 Working from the right side of the fabric insert the needle slightly to the side of the area to be stitched, pull the needle back up ready for the first cross-stitch, leaving a short length of thread at the front of the embroidery. Work several stitches, catching the thread at the back as you sew, and then cut off the remainder of the loose end at the back of the work.

1 Make a knot in the thread and bring the needle up from the back of the fabric, ready for the first stitch, leave a small length of thread at the back of the embroidery and feeling the knot so to keep it in place, work several stitches to anchor the thread and then cut off any loose ends.

LOOPED START

Sometimes it is necessary to make a very small, isolated area of stitching when working on individual motifs, such as a bee or a sprig of leaves and a simple method for securing the first stitch is to pass the needle through a loop on the reverse of the fabric.

1 Cut a single length of thread about twice as long as you usually work with and double it over, and then thread the needle with the two cut ends. Bring the needle up from the back of the fabric, leaving the looped end on the wrong side, return the needle after making the first stitch and pass it through the open loop to secure the stitch.

1 An alternative method that is sometimes useful when working with a single thread, is to make a very small looped knot at the end of the thread and pass the needle back through this loop to anchor the first stitch.

LENGTH OF THREADS

The ideal length for stranded embroidery cottons is about 46cm or 18 inches, although quite often a thread may start to look a bit dull and lifeless before you have come to the end of the length. If this should happen it is best to stop working with it and start afresh, as not only will the thread appear to be thinner and provide less cover on the fabric but also it will cause the colour to change slightly. Sometimes I have been tempted to carry on, but I always end up unpicking the stitches and wasting my time.

Rayon threads should be cut to about the same length of 46 cm (18 inches) but can be used in slightly longer lengths although they are more liable to twist and tangle if you are not careful.

1 Metallic threads have a tendency to fray quite easily and have to be treated more carefully. Shorter lengths of about 36 cm (14 inches) are more practicable but the delicate fibres can occasionally separate and appear fluffy and tired, in which case you should start again with a new thread.

STICH TECHNIQUES

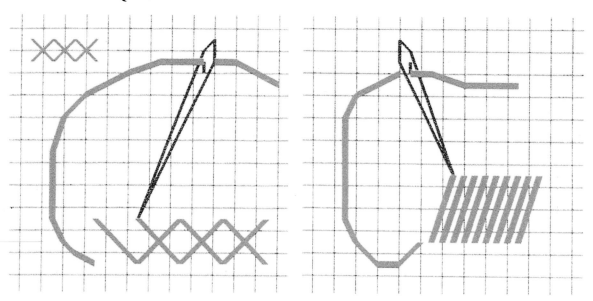

Cross-stitch Stitches can be completed individually or worked in rows of half-crosses in one direction, and then returned. Petit-point is a smaller stitch over a single thread.

Satin-stitch Stitches can be worked in an upright or slanted position, but should all follow the same direction and lay close enough together to cover the fabric.

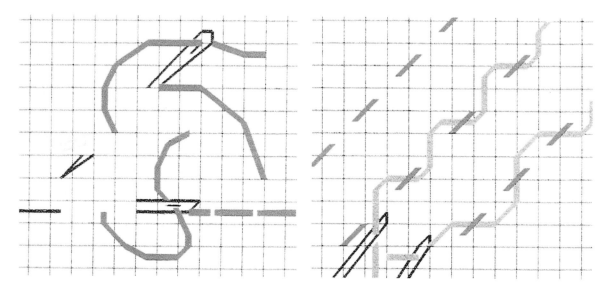

Back-stitch A series of stitches worked forwards and backwards to form a complete line, which can be made in small evenly sized lengths or in a series of random lengths..

Running-stitch A series of evenly spaced stitches, that are worked over and under the fabric. A line of thread can be woven through the stitches to create a Whip-stitch.

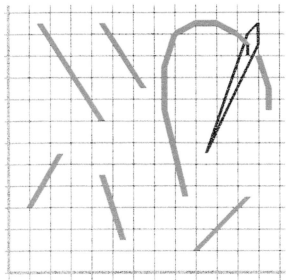

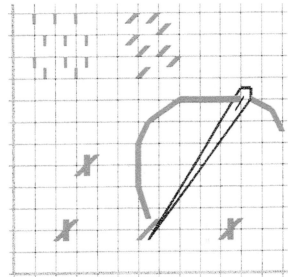

Straight-stitches These stitches can be made to any length and placed in any direction.
A series of stitches placed next to each other, can be built up to cover an entire area.

Seed-stitch These small straight stitches can be reworked several times to create a raised surface or the top stitch can be placed at a slight angle to the lower stitch.

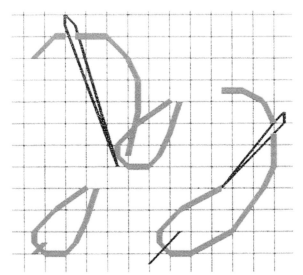

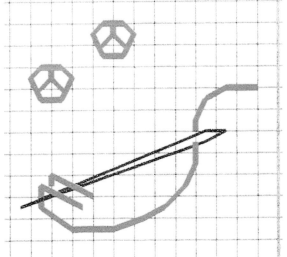

Lazy-daisy A decorative looped stitch, that can be worked in one or two threads. The length can be varied slightly, but the small anchor stitch should be kept close to the loop.

French-knot The size of the stitch can be varied according to the number of times the thread is twisted round the needle. Keep the threads pulled tight as the knot is worked.

CHAPTER TWO
buildings

Apart from a few notable examples, buildings were not generally included in samplers until about the middle of the 18th century, when the pictorial style of sampler emerged, and picturesque compositions displaying a period country house, surrounded by trees and flowers became an extremely popular subject choice. Some of the earliest recorded buildings are featured in a series of band samplers dating from the 1660's, all of which depict a large manor house standing beside a formal knot garden, and an example of this design can be seen in the sampler by Margaret Mason, in the Victoria & Albert Museum. In each embroidery the building is outlined in a double running-stitch, although the version by Elizabeth Sexton, in the collection of Witney Antiques, includes an area of stitching that represents a brickwork pattern, and also a darker area that perhaps suggests a timber framed building or stonework. A third sampler, from the Fitzwilliam Collection, has an additional pictorial band which includes a large oak tree with figure, and what appears to be an imposing gate-house. The inspiration for these unusual sampler patterns is attributed to the much publicised account of Charles II's restoration, and illustrates the house and tree in which he took refuge. The three designs are so alike in their composition and colouring, that it seems they may have all been worked from the same basic pattern, and might possibly have originated from a particular school or tutor.

During the remainder of the 17th century buildings still appear only occasionally in samplers, although there are a number of examples in both Dutch and German embroideries from that period, where small buildings have been included in the design. In the main samplers continued to be worked within the same basic format, comprising of a collection of narrow bands of patterns, however two other styles of embroidery were to have a major influence on the development of the sampler. Firstly the art of canvas-work, which used a simple tent-stitch technique to produce embroideries full of highly animated compositions, depicting figures, buildings and animals set in rural and pastoral scenes, and secondly the naturalistic style of the needle art pictures that employed crewel-work techniques to create imaginative and expressive individual interpretations. By the middle of the 18th century both of these vibrant and picturesque styles were already being adapted and absorbed into the traditional sampler format, with the effect that the sampler became wider and more square in shape, in order to contain a series of pictorial motifs and scenes, placed within a decorative border

A significant example that ideally reflects this period of change is evident in a sampler dated 1752, by Elizabeth Cridland, and displayed in the Victoria & Albert Museum. The top section of the embroidery is mainly made up of a collection of basic spot motifs, arranged in a symmetrical format and quite typical of patterns that were in general use at the time. However, across the full width of the lower section of the sampler there is a significant and striking pictorial landscape that includes two buildings and a windmill, connected by a large expanse of grass, suggesting fields and hillocks. The simple and unsophisticated style of the composition has a charming naïve quality, and yet this scene depicting an unpretentious house, line of fencing dotted with fir trees, leading to a birdhouse and small garden building is almost identical to the basic design for the enchanting House and Barn samplers that were so fashionable in the New England states of Portsmouth during the early 19th century. The style and arrangement of the motifs is so similar, that one wonders whether the idea for this appealing little composition somehow found its way to the Americas.

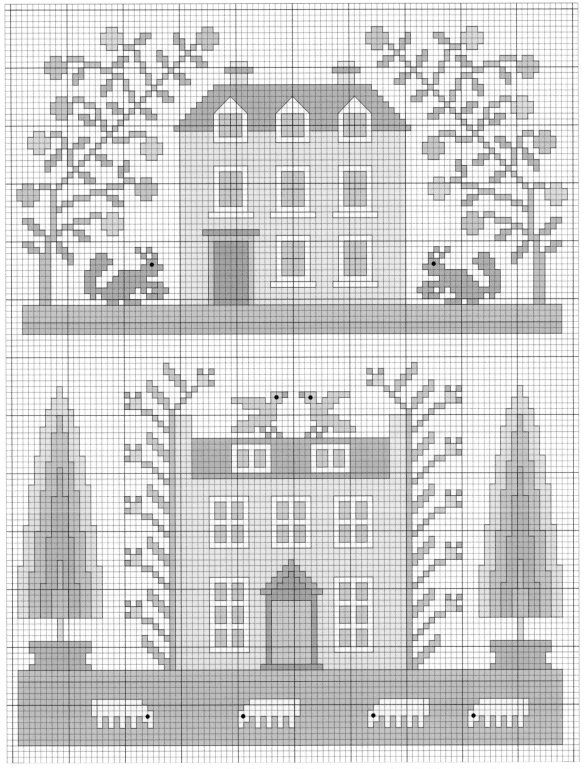

Flowering shrubs, potted plants and occasionally a motif that represented a climbing rose, all made attractive decorative features in the traditional house and garden composition, and the style and arrangement of the various motifs could be adapted to suit the proportions of a particular building.

GEORGIAN HOUSES

The new architectural styles that were emerging in England by the beginning of the 18th century, were to have an enormous influence on the growing interest in pictorial sampler embroidery. The classical style, of the elegant and perfectly proportioned buildings, was a source of inspiration for the idealised version of an imposing country house, which was to become a feature of so many schoolroom samplers. The basic pattern for a simple square building, with large windows and framed doorway, provided a wealth of possibilities for individual interpretation, and variations on the style of the roof, size and position of windows and shape of doorframe, were to engage and enthuse the embroiderer endlessly. The traditional ideal of the red brick house was depicted in numerous colour variations, with shades ranging from pale brown, to pink and bright red, and the white or ecru colours used to represent the brick bonding made a particularly decorative overall pattern. The majority of buildings in English samplers were worked in natural earth colours, and in many cases would reflect the style of architecture in the region, and this is particularly evident in Scottish samplers, where the very distinctive interpretation of the local buildings is easily recognisable. In general, the fabrics used for samplers were finely woven linens, and the small scale of the stitches made it possible to work the whole design in cross-stitch, including details for windows, door frames and brickwork patterns. However, occasionally back-stitch techniques were used to describe additional features, as the delicate line of the single thread was particularly suitable for depicting fine details, such as window frames and glazing bars, especially on smaller houses.

The pattern and colour scheme for this design is on page 100.

The traditional schoolroom sampler often featured a symmetrical arrangement of motifs with a large house placed in a central position. However many other examples displayed a more random approach with sometimes two or more buildings arranged in various positions within the composition.

COLONIAL HOUSES

The wide variety of architectural styles that sprung up in the newly emerging states of colonial America, were originally influenced by the broad and diverse heritage of the European settlers, and the growing fascination and preoccupation with the subject of buildings was gradually reflected in the pictorial needlework samplers, that were to become a compulsory part of an education for young girls. It is impossible to know how many of the buildings featured in the embroideries were actual representations of the family home, or were simply motifs adapted from standard patterns, but certainly some of the more distinctive designs can be traced to well known public buildings or schools. The house motif was to appear on samplers in every style imaginable, ranging from small saltbox cottages to grand colonial mansions, and the wealth and complexity of the subject included not only the huge variations in architectural styles between the different regions, but also the individual interpretations and artistic styles of the various schools.

A typical composition of a large house positioned between two stylised trees, was made all the more appealing by the attractive patterns of the little rows of fencing that encircled the lawns full of animals and figures, and helped establish this imaginative and vibrant style of embroidery as a distinctive and unique art form.

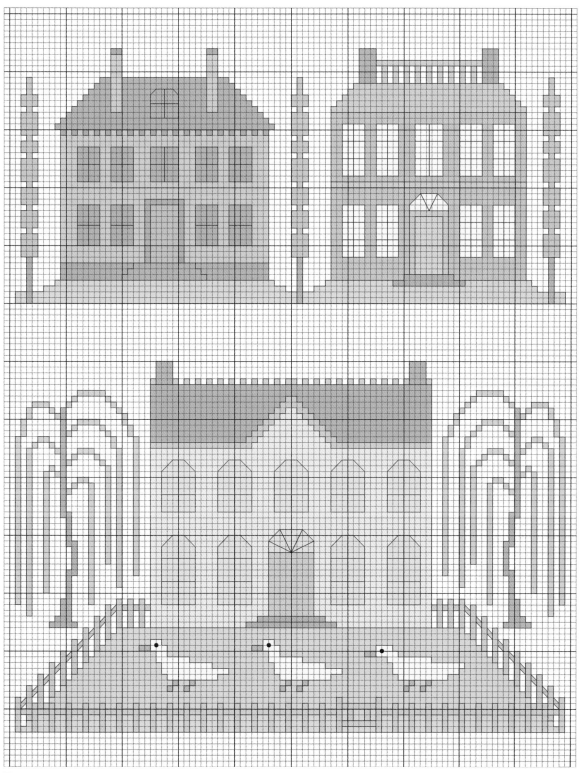

The large colonial house with its many windows, wide doorways and expansive lawns was an ever popular subject choice for the pictorial sampler. These bright and colourful embroidered houses, often reflected the original colours of the painted weatherboarding on earlier buildings.

A number of samplers feature buildings in varying shades of deep red, and these attractive colour schemes may well have reflected the actual colour of a particular building. The range of coloured threads available was probably very limited, but these bold statements lend added charm to the embroidery.

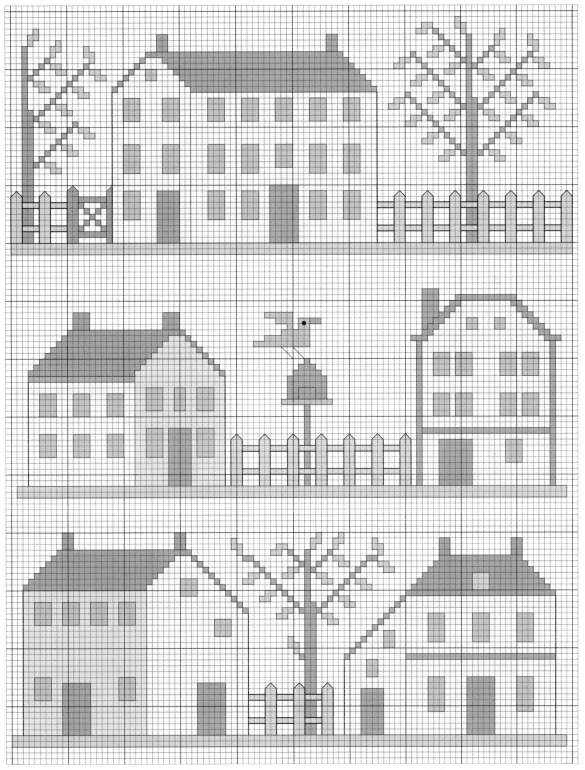

Many variations on this style of building feature in American samplers throughout the nineteenth century. The distinctive motifs were based on the architectural designs used in the early Quaker settlements, and the rows of little green windows represent the wooden shutters on the original buildings.

This simple brickwork design is ideally suited to the scale of a smaller building, and makes a very effective overall pattern. Sometimes the bricks were arranged in larger blocks, with a set of four stitches to each square.

A combination of petit-point and standard cross-stitch techniques, have been used to create the attractive stone-work pattern on this little cottage. The fine lines of the cream coloured bonding, enhance the subdued colouring of the stone. The patterns and colour schemes for these designs are on page 101.

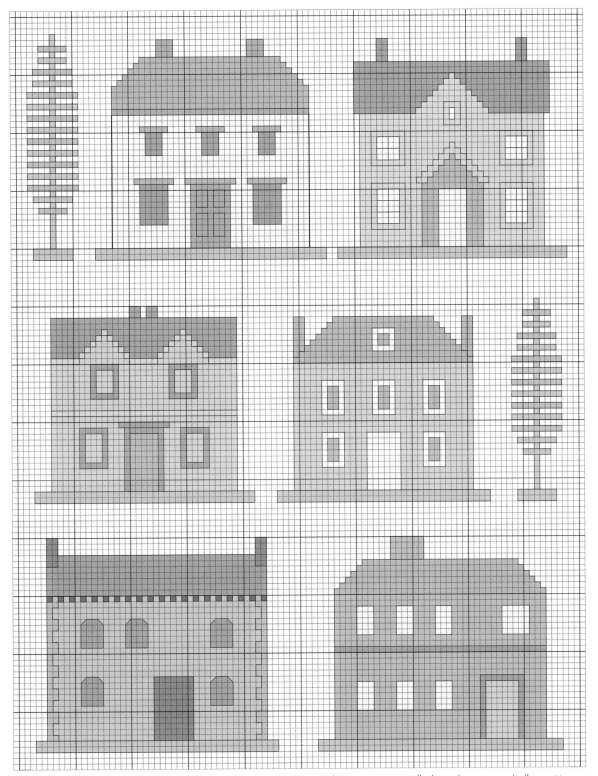

Small cottage style buildings appear in numerous samplers and many are actually based on very similar patterns. The character of a building can be altered very easily by simply changing the size and arrangement of the windows, position of the doorway, and outline of the roof.

CHURCHES

Commemorative samplers that celebrate special events such as births, christenings and marriages have been a particular feature of the late 20th century, and continue to be popular to this day. A picturesque composition, portraying the family church, surrounded by floral motifs and associated themes, together with an inscription including names and dates, provides a wonderful keepsake of a memorable occasion.

The family church features in this detail from a commemorative christening sampler, which also includes stylised yew trees and a pair of doves trailing garlands of flowers.

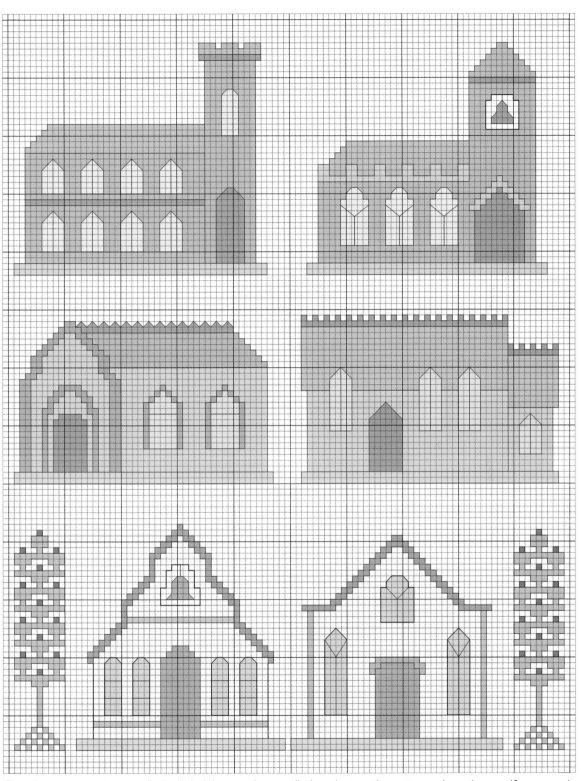

Churches were not generally included in samplers until the nineteenth century, when the motif appears in connection with a number of different themes including, notable examples of architecture, the village or school church, and occasionally a church or chapel featured in a mourning sampler.

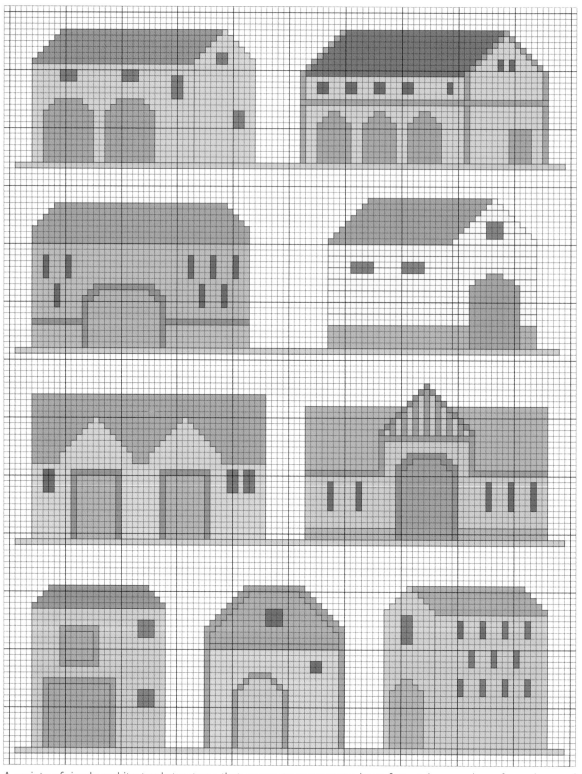

A variety of simple architectural structures that appear to represent a barn, feature in a number of samplers, and although they are sometimes part of a village scene, they are more usually included in farm related themes, and always bring added interest and character to the composition.

Little scenes depicting farmsteads were very popular, and this array of small barns, outhouses and cottages, has been inspired by the charming House and Barn samplers from New Hampshire, and a delightful rural composition from an English sampler in the collection of the Gloucester Folk Museum.

CHAPTER THREE
figures

Throughout the course of sampler history the human figure has remained one of the most captivating and intriguing choices of subject, and whether portrayed as a single figure or group of figures engaged in an activity, the various actions, dress and relationship between the characters, gives the embroidery an instant appeal and attraction. The wonderful array of costumed figures that appear in sampler compositions, reflect the many changes and developments in styles of dress and clothing, with each period in time represented by motifs of various figures attired in contemporary fashions. There are a number of examples of little figures appearing in early band samplers, and although these embroideries were primarily concerned with the recording of stitch techniques and repeat border patterns, motifs based on religious and patriotic themes were often included alongside the floral designs.

Amongst the more common motifs and themes that frequently appeared in early samplers, were the stylised boxer figures that seemed to represent a universal motif of a male figure that could be continually changed and adapted to suit any situation. The small rows of little men carrying their flowering trophies have appeared in many forms and guises, ranging from almost naked to full contemporary dress. Likewise the ever popular biblical scene depicting the figures of Adam and Eve, has been interpreted in an endless variety of compositions, and the many variations on the amount and style of any clothing has probably been influenced by changing attitudes to the naked figure. Several band samplers from the first half of the 17th century, include variations on a basic pattern for a little scene depicting three ladies dressed in elaborate costumes, that were typical of the highly decorative garments from the Tudor era. The central figure of the group is thought to represent Queen Elizabeth 1, with her ladies in waiting standing either side of her, and the stylised dress patterns were often embellished with beads and spangles together with ornate headdresses and decorative fans. The motifs were often worked in deep reds and blues, and there is a lovely example of this most interesting and fascinating of compositions, in the collection of Witney Antiques. As the new century progressed the emerging fashion styles of the Stuart period became more established, and a number of samplers include pictorial scenes depicting a man and a woman standing together, dressed in garments that displayed the latest attire. A detailed example of the type of clothing worn in the first half of the 17th century, features in a sampler by Elizabeth Short, in the Victoria and Albert Museum. A second example worked by Anne Lawle, is in the Fitzwilliam Museum, and features a similar composition with a more naturalistically styled figure dressed as a Royalist Cavalier, doffing his hat to a lady in a long flowing gown.

The 18th century saw yet more changes, as pictorial compositions began to include little figures engaged in everyday activities, and the various motifs portraying farmers, shepherds and milkmaids were probably inspired by the designs in Dutch and German pattern books. Another important development towards the second half of the century was the interest in the family portrait composition, which featured members of the family together with the family house and grounds. A wonderful example in the Goodhart Collection and dated 1778, depicts an intimate family group with several children, all dressed in the new flowing styles of the Regency period. At about the same time, a number of American schools began to produce embroideries based on a similar theme, and groups of figures that possibly represented family members, were to feature in a series of the most appealing and engaging sampler compositions.

The pastoral scene of a shepherd and his flock has always been a favourite subject in English samplers, whereas an interest in agricultural and farming practises features in numerous American embroideries, and reflects the rural lifestyle of the farmstead, that was common to so many families.

These animated scenes of figures at work are typical of a country lifestyle, and represent the various activities that have been taking place for generations. The little scene of apple-pickers was inspired by a design on a late sixteenth-century cushion in the collection of the Victoria and Albert Museum.

Small cottage garden scenes depicting various figures engaged in outdoor activities are equally relevant in samplers today. Buildings can be quite easily adapted and altered, to resemble a particular house, and styles of dress and clothing can be updated to create a contemporary reference.

Motifs depicting figures involved in domestic activities and village life have always played a part in traditional Dutch and German samplers. Everyday events such as milking, butter-making and drawing water from the well, often featured alongside patterns for stylised flowers arrangements.

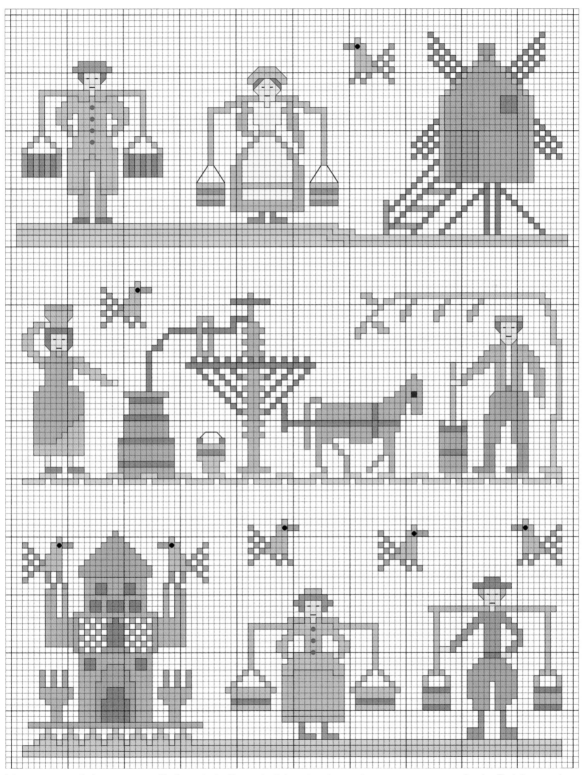

Numerous variations on motifs for windmills and elaborate dovecotes were very popular in Dutch samplers, together with smaller motifs for a milkmaid, carrying a yoke and pails. Rural scenes that featured the farmer and his wife, tending a horse-drawn mill, were more unusual.

TUDOR FIGURES

The exaggerated styles and ornate decoration of the fashions from the Tudor era, have been captured perfectly in an intriguing example of a group of three Elizabethan figures, that feature in a mid-17th-century sampler from the Goodhart Collection, and together with the example previously referred to at the beginning of the chapter, they make a fascinating subject for further interpretation. The endless possibilities for embellishing and decorating the large, over-sized gowns, with various beads, sequins and metallic threads provides a wonderful opportunity for imaginative and creative innovation.

The patterns and colour schemes for these motifs feature on page 102

The decorative costumes from the Tudor and Stuart period were to provide an ideal source of inspiration for the many styles of contemporary dress, that feature in a number of seventeenth-century samplers, and a range of intricate stitches and metallic threads were used to describe the finer details.

COMMEMORATIVE SAMPLERS.

Although the traditional sampler does not appear to commemorate a special event such as a wedding, with a specific pictorial composition, the family record sampler featured the full names of both husband and wife, together with their marriage dates, followed by the names and dates of birth, and in some cases deaths, of all the children. This type of embroidery was quite common during the 18th century and the examples that have survived, provide a valuable and poignant piece of social history.

The pattern and colour scheme for this design features on page 103.

The idea of making a gift sampler to celebrate a particular occasion such as a marriage, engagement or anniversary has become a favourite subject for the embroiderer in recent times. A picturesque scene portraying the marriage ceremony, with the bride and groom surrounded by various related motifs, including garlands of flowers, little birds and perhaps family members, together with names and dates makes a lovely item of memorabilia for future generations.

Festivals and celebrations with displays of traditional customs, including folk-dancing and performances, have always been a part of every culture, and Dutch samplers in particular feature a variety of patterns and motifs depicting decorative hearts and flowers, to symbolise the marriage ceremony.

CHAPTER FOUR

trees

Some of the first recorded examples of a tree motif being used in sampler embroidery, appear in two 16th century embroideries, in the collection of the Victoria and Albert Museum. Both embroideries depict variations on the same type of pattern, and in the earliest example which originates from Germany, there is a highly stylised version of a design for a large pomegranate tree sheltering a bird, which represented the motif titled Pelican in Piety, and as such held particular symbolic and religious significance. The second sampler dated 1598 is Jane Bostocke's well documented embroidery and includes tree motifs relating to a similar theme, although they appear to be based on very early Dutch patterns, which she may have acquired from a travelling relative, as they were probably not in general circulation at that time. However, Jane has also included various family emblems in the composition, and places a squirrel on one tree and an owl in the centre of the smaller tree, which appears to add a humorous touch to the design and gives it a distinctly English reference. This particular style of tree motif has occasionally been adapted to resemble an oak tree pattern, as the large leaves and small fruit have a number of similarities.

On the whole, trees that featured in samplers during the 17th century were included in the little pictorial scenes that occasionally occurred in band samplers, alongside the rows of floral patterns. Designs for figurative motifs were usually depicted in a naturalistic style, as many of the patterns were copied from contemporary woodcuts, which were then transferred onto the fabric and further adapted and personalised by the embroiderer. Two samplers from the Burrell Collection perfectly illustrate the style of embroidery in use during this period, and in a sampler dated 1663, the technique of double running-stitch has been used to illustrate a decorative pattern for a large oak tree, which appears in a small scene that includes a male figure and some animals. In the second sampler dated 1668, a pair of very pretty and delicately worked fruit trees, stand either side of a costumed figure in a garden scene, all of which have been worked in a variety of techniques.

By the following century the stylised motifs from the Netherlands and Germany were becoming more readily available as printed patterns, and the attractive cross-stitch designs began to appear with regular frequency in English samplers. A range of decorative motifs for stylised trees, with several birds perched amongst the branches, were widely used in European samplers, together with distinctive patterns for various fruit-bearing trees, including brightly coloured lemon and orange trees and many of these designs were later adapted to represent apple and cherry trees in the English school-room embroideries. With the focus on the more aesthetic and pleasing aspects of the pictorial sampler, less importance was being placed on any religious and symbolic references, although the enduring popularity of the composition depicting the figures of Adam and Eve, standing beneath the fruit laden Tree of Knowledge, remained a favourite subject and became an ideal way of introducing a colourful and decorative element into the design.

However, another outside influence was to affect the style and content of the sampler embroidery and gradually introduce a more expressive and creative approach to the subject. The growing trade links between Europe and the Far East during the 17th century, resulted in an influx of textiles in the form of printed fabrics and carpets all bearing free-flowing, naturalistic designs, worked in bright, vibrant colours. In England this novel and exciting decorative style was readily adapted and absorbed alongside the more formal cross-stitch patterns, but it was in the New England colonies, where sampler embroidery was just beginning to develop its own individual identity that a new and highly imaginative style began to emerge.

The varying shapes of the irregular leaf patterns combine to make a very attractive design and the distinctive style of this large oak tree, with its broad leaves and waving branches was inspired by a most unusual tree motif in a sampler dated 1808, in the collection of Witney Antiques.

The oak became a symbol of patriotism during the seventeenth century and was sometimes featured as the Royal Oak, supporting three crowns. However, many samplers depict the large tree as home to various owls and squirrels, placing the little animals amongst its spreading branches.

40

Formal patterns for various fruiting trees appear frequently in both Dutch and English samplers and decorative designs combining oak leaf and acorn motifs were amongst the most popular. Arches and bowers bearing fruits, flowers and leaf patterns were often used as a symbol of celebration.

TREES

The combined influences of the various stylised tree patterns from Asia, and the 17th century passion for topiary, were soon reflected in the embroidery designs of the period and motifs for simple cone shaped trees began to appear with increasing regularity. As the trend towards making a pictorial scene rather than a record of patterns, became more established, a most attractive composition depicting a stylised house flanked by two symmetrical pyramid shaped trees gained in popularity, and was to eventually become one of the most enduring images associated with the sampler. The wide appeal of this particular subject and the simplicity of the overall design, meant that the house and garden format was reproduced endlessly throughout the school-room period, and subsequently there are innumerable variations on these basic tree patterns in a range of different styles and colour combinations.

Trees in general are probably one of the most versatile and adaptable of subjects to work with, allowing the embroiderer the opportunity to change and alter a motif to any shape, size or style required, in order to fit the pattern into a particular space in a composition. Quite apart from the individual characteristics of the various species, the basic tree shape is so easily recognisable that there are few limitations to its possibilities and even the most simple outline of a stem and foliage will create an impression of a tree.

This detail from a Family Portrait sampler depicts four young brothers playing beneath a row of Beech trees. A range of green, yellow and brown threads have been mixed and blended together to create a sense of light and movement amongst the areas of foliage.

The simple geometric shapes and angular forms of the cone-shaped tree pattern were ideally suited to interpretation in cross-stitch, and soon became one of the main components of the school-room sampler, with numerous permutations and variations in existence.

CONE SHAPED TREES

Although cross-stitch was the simplest and most popular technique for depicting this style of tree, there are a number of examples in both English and American samplers, where the use of various techniques such as satin-stitch, long-stitch or French knots has resulted in a more expressive and individual interpretation. In general colours varied from dark green-blue, to lighter greens and browns, and in many instances were probably determined by the limited range of colours available at any one time.

The patterns and colour schemes for these designs feature on page 104.

The traditional form of the pyramid pattern more closely resembled a topiary tree, with a dense area of colour that covered the entire shape, but in other examples the motif is arranged in a more open structure and is sometimes worked in a geometric diamond-shaped pattern.

WILLOW TREES

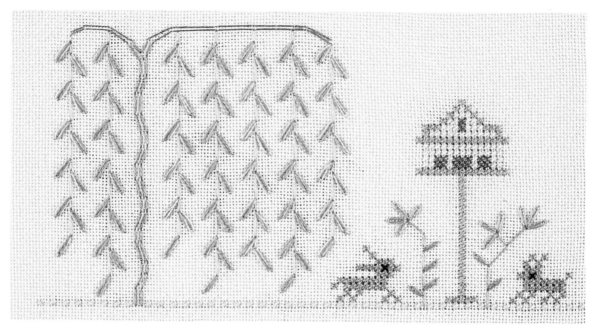

An impression of the gentle swaying motion of the willow tree can be achieved by using two different colours in the needle, as the variations in the twists and turns of the threads creates a sense of movement.

The graceful and picturesque qualities of the weeping willow are ideally suited to interpretation through a more naturalistic and expressive style of stitch technique. The patterns and colour schemes for these designs feature on page 105.

The long drooping branches of the willow, appear to give the tree a melancholy air and in embroidery the willow motif was very popular as a symbol of loss and sorrow. A composition depicting a tombstone overhung with willow boughs, features on a number of mourning samplers.

WILLOW TREES

A completely different style of motif can be created, by using straight stitch techniques to describe the delicate qualities of the willow boughs.

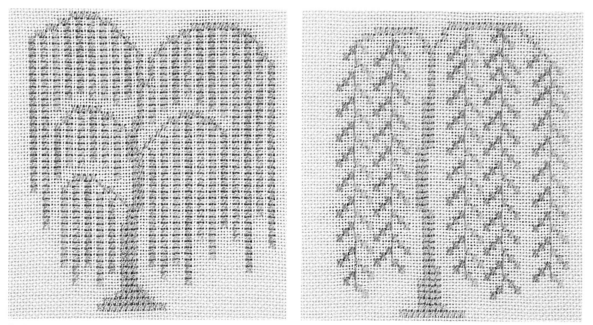

Stylised motifs worked in cross-stitch, can be further enhanced by using different shades of blue, yellow and green, to create interest and variation. The patterns and colour schemes for these designs feature on page 106.

The characteristic long thin leaves and slender branches of the willow, makes this tree a particularly challenging motif to interpret in embroidery. There have been a number of different approaches to the subject, ranging from stylised cross-stitch designs to more creative free flowing examples.

There are numerous patterns for different types and styles of fruiting trees and certain motifs appear more recognisable than others. Colours were often selected according to their aesthetic value and availability, with some motifs displaying several varieties of fruit on the one tree.

Stylised trees bearing small fruits or berries often appear in Scottish samplers and could easily be adapted to fit a required space. The unusual design of the central motif could possibly resemble a holly tree, and was inspired by an English sampler dated 1766 in the collection of Witney Antiques.

CHAPTER FIVE

animals and birds

The growing interest in the subject of natural history, following the first expeditions to the New World in the 16th century, resulted in a series of publications describing and illustrating the newly discovered species of plants and animals. Initially several books were produced, which were intended as a serious scientific record, but the simple designs of the attractively coloured woodcuts were so appealing and engaging, that they were soon being used as a source of reference material for needlework. By the turn of the century, pattern books aimed directly at the embroiderer were being published in rapid succession and advances in printing methods meant that more detailed designs could be reproduced using copper plate printing techniques. Editions with long descriptive titles such as 'One book of Birds sitting on Sprigs' and another dated 1671 had a title beginning 'Four Hundred new sorts of Birds, Beasts' and ending 'for all sorts of Gentlewomen and School Mistresses Works', which suggests that even at this early date similar patterns were now being made available to a much wider audience.

Throughout the history of textiles, motifs for birds and animals have always remained a firm favourite with the embroiderer, and since the importance of proportion has always been of little significance in the context of the sampler, this has meant that motifs for small and large animals could sit comfortably side by side without appearing incongruous. In this way birds, rabbits, squirrels, deer and insects could all occupy the same amount of space in the composition and be arranged together in a design according to the embroiderers preference, rather than having to refer to their relative size in reality.

There is a huge range of patterns in existence for motifs depicting various species of birds, and although there are numerous individual interpretations they can be roughly divided into several main groups, including large exotic birds, small garden birds, domestic fowl, wild fowl and birds of prey. Various types of birds are featured in the earliest recorded samplers and although many of the original patterns were often based on heraldic emblems for subjects, such as the Pelican, Eagle and Swan, it was the colourful green Woodpecker that was to become one of the most popular motifs in early English samplers, and was invariably included in a variety of floral patterns, the most common being a repeat border design. Garden birds in general were not always distinguishable and were usually worked in various shades of brown, but the Robin is often singled out for his distinctive colouring as is the pretty Bluebird, which appears frequently in American compositions. The numerous patterns for a slightly larger more stylised motif, were usually based on exotic species such as the parrot family and include variations on Parakeets, Cockatoos and Toucans, and also the Bird of Paradise and Golden Pheasant, which all provided a wonderful source of inspiration for colourful and decorative interpretations.

The majority of bird patterns were worked in cross-stitch, especially the more common motifs that were used in school-room situations but there are many other highly individual and imaginative examples, where crewel-work techniques have been used to add detailed markings and patterns to the design, creating a more naturalistic style of motif. The inclusion of small birds in a sampler is often used as a decorative device, with the more pictorial compositions showing birds in flight or perched on trees, and this can often add a humorous and amusing touch to the scene. This is particularly the case in some of the north American samplers from New Jersey, where a huge array of animated birds adorn trees, houses, fences and gates, all seeming to bring character and individual charm to the scene.

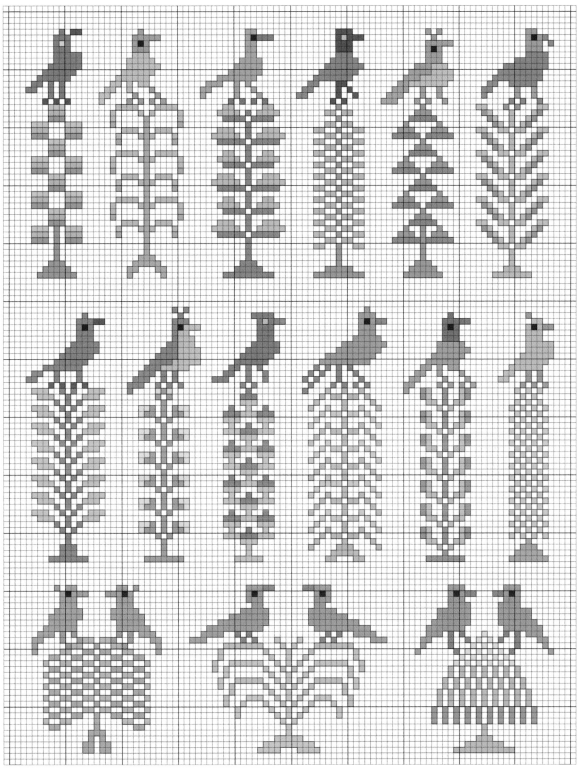

Small stylised tree motifs with a bird perched on the top branches, are very common as space-fillers in many samplers. The simple repeat patterns used to depict the leaves and branches are most effective, and open to endless permutations and variation in both the colour and the design.

A combination of decorative designs and colourful patterns were often used to depict the individual markings on various types of birds, and although it is sometimes possible to recognise a particular species, the majority of patterns were probably just imaginative interpretations.

Motifs depicting various birds pecking and snatching at fruit-laden trees, always adds a touch of amusement and humour to a design, and the random arrangement of the brightly coloured fruit makes an attractive backdrop, for any assortment of stylised or naturalistic bird patterns.

PEACOCKS

The peacock represents pride, vanity and extravagance and appears in early embroideries as a symbol of immortality, although it was probably more often selected for its attractive and colourful decorative qualities, which combine to make it such an appealing subject. Patterns for several highly stylised motifs were appearing in Dutch samplers from as early as the 17th century, with a range of designs depicting the tail feathers in a variety of fan shaped arrangements. Another particularly attractive collection of stylised patterns originated from Germany and are possibly from an earlier period. Variations on a basic motif for a very large and imposing peacock, feature in a number of early German embroideries with a variety of lively colour combinations, including bright blues, pinks and yellows together with shades of brown and dark

green, and there are two good examples in the collection of Witney Antiques. Motifs depicting the peacock are quite common in English samplers and although they were generally based on a range of Dutch patterns, others examples displayed a more individual interpretation, with a combination of cross-stitch and crewelwork techniques being employed to illustrate the decorative tail feathers. The many similarities between Dutch and Scottish patterns is probably due to the strong trade links between the two countries during the 17th century, and this may account for the popularity of the peacock motif in Scottish embroideries. Several motifs depicting the peacock in a variety of poses might appear in the one composition, and occasionally the decorative birds are featured adorning the rooftops of a large country house.

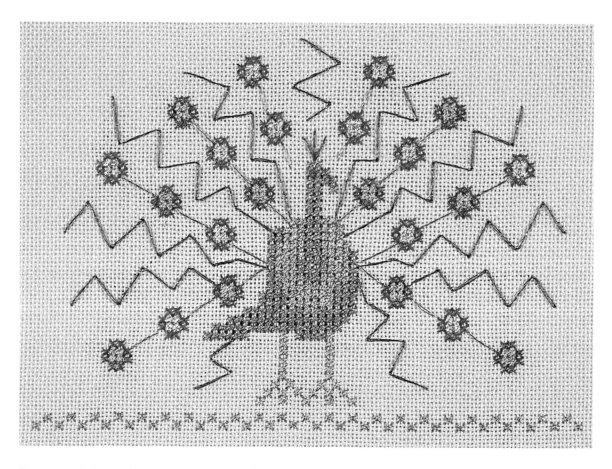

The open design and simple arrangement of the decorative tail feathers has been further highlighted with a combination of lustre and metallic threads. The pattern and colour scheme for this design feature on page 107.

There are several standard stylised designs in existence for the peacock motif, with any amount of variations on these basic patterns. The very decorative and colourful display of tail feathers provides a wonderful opportunity for imaginative and individual interpretations.

ANIMALS

Many of the animal and bird motifs that were used in sampler embroidery had specific symbolic meanings that originated from classical literature and mythology, while patterns for certain animals were also based on heraldic symbols and included mythical beasts, such as the unicorn and dragon. The presence of a particular animal in the embroidery, would convey a meaningful message to the viewer and this method of descriptive imagery was often used to illustrate Christian beliefs, as for example the significance of the motif depicting the Pelican in Piety or the Serpent in the Garden of Eden. Although many of these patterns were to remain in use for over a century, the actual significance of their meaning was to become less important and gradually many motifs were selected purely for their aesthetic and decorative values.

The inclusion of small animals such as rabbits and squirrels was gaining in popularity during the seventeenth century, and the rabbit or hare features prominently in many Scottish sampler compositions. Motifs depicting the impish red squirrel were to become a firm favourite in English embroideries, and there are a number of patterns showing this endearing little creature either scampering amongst the treetops or invariably sitting with a small fruit or nut. The more unusual example of the little black squirrel is sometimes represented on German samplers, together with a motif for a black rabbit and also a very striking black speckled cockerel. Although there are several patterns for cats in existence, they only appear very rarely on samplers and more usually on the earlier embroideries, whereas patterns for dogs are quite common and there are various motifs depicting them both as hunting dogs and also as a family pet.

The dog named Juno in Jane Bostocke's sampler is portrayed in quite a naturalistic style, which seems closer to the type of illustration found on the table carpets of that period, rather than the formal stylised patterns of the tree motifs, in her embroidery. There is also a motif for a very similar breed of dog, together with a larger type of guard dog, that both appear in an English spot sampler dated 1630, in the collection of the Dorset County Museum, so perhaps there were already some patterns in existence for a range of domestic animals. Motifs depicting small stylised dogs became very common during the 18th century, and as samplers became more personalised the House and Garden sampler often featured a group of figures that possibly represented the family, accompanied by the pet dog. Scenes such as this were particularly popular in American compositions and sometimes included a little dog standing next to his kennel.

The interest in farm animals and rural activities was primarily a subject that featured in Dutch samplers, and small scenes depicting a Milkmaid with Cow, or a Horse turning the wheels for the Churn, were typical examples from a range of motifs that illustrated farming practices at that time. English samplers generally appear to include fewer designs that reflect a rustic lifestyle, and although motifs for cows, occasionally horses and very rarely pigs, do sometimes feature in an embroidery, it was usually the more picturesque landscape scenes that were aspired to. The perfect rural idyll of grazing sheep, accompanied by basking deer and rabbits came to personify the landed gentry and their country estates, in a calm and pleasing manner. Many of the American samplers also include farm animals and related motifs, but the often haphazard arrangement of the cows, sheep, dogs, domestic fowl and figures usually conveys a very lively and energetic scene, with a number of the motifs worked in a more naturalistic style.

Squirrel motifs were particularly common in pictorial samplers and were probably included for their picturesque qualities. However, in earlier pieces they were often portrayed in a more realistic style and their appearance may have been a deliberate reference to the theme of mischief.

DEER

The deer was considered the Royal beast of the hunt and signified the huge importance attached to the sport of hunting during the 16th century. There are several early patterns for a stag with large antlers depicted in a reclining position, and although canvas-work compositions illustrating the hunt were very popular during this period, the majority of samplers have portrayed the deer as a calm and restful animal, and they were often positioned standing near to a tree. There are two almost identical designs for a small rural scene, depicting a figure of possibly a gamekeeper or hunter standing in a green field, surrounded by four stags and some rabbits. Both embroideries date from the first quarter of the 17th century, and one example is in the Victoria and Albert Museum, and the other in the Burrell Collection at the Glasgow Museum. A band sampler from the same era, and part of the Goodhart Collection, also includes a hunting theme and depicts a figure of an archer aiming his arrow into a forest of flowering plants and animals. Pictorial hunting scenes are generally not very common, as perhaps the subject was not thought of as being very suitable for young girls, but there are a number of patterns that appear in Scottish samplers which depict a rather decorative and stylised hunt scene, with the figure of a man aiming his gun at a group of little rabbits sitting on mounds of grass. An example of this unusual composition is illustrated in a sampler dated 1812, in the collection of Witney Antiques.

Rural scenes including small hillocks and strips of grass, worked with both cross-stitch and straight-stitch techniques, were a colourful and attractive addition to many compositions. The patterns and colour schemes for this design feature on page 108.

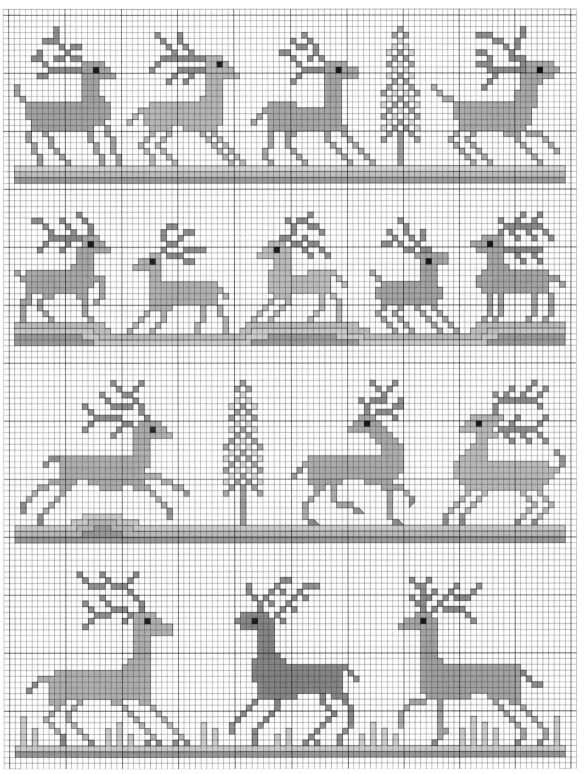

The stag with spreading antlers is regarded as the symbol of the hunt, and although relatively few samplers have included compositions depicting a hunting scene, the attractive and varied patterns of the antlers makes these graceful creatures a very interesting and popular subject.

HENS AND GEESE

Motifs depicting cockerels, hens, ducks, geese and swans were especially common in Dutch samplers, particularly during the 18th century, and there are some patterns for a very large brightly coloured cockerel that appear on several German samplers from that period. On the whole motifs for domestic fowl were not used very often in English samplers, although a pattern for a large swan that dates from a 16th century pattern book, has occasionally appeared in early band samplers and is sometimes depicted as the Royal swan, bearing a crown on its head. The English pictorial compositions that included a large house standing on an expanse of green, dotted with sheep and sometimes deer, were intended to represent the fields and land of a country estate, and on the whole were quite formal in appearance. However, in contrast to this many of the pictorial scenes depicted in American embroideries, illustrate a more intimate and personalised style, with the emphasis being on farming rather than parkland. These colourful country house scenes included grassy lawns populated with domestic fowl of all shapes and sizes, so that hens, cockerels and geese competed with dogs, sheep, cows and figures for space on a crowded plot.

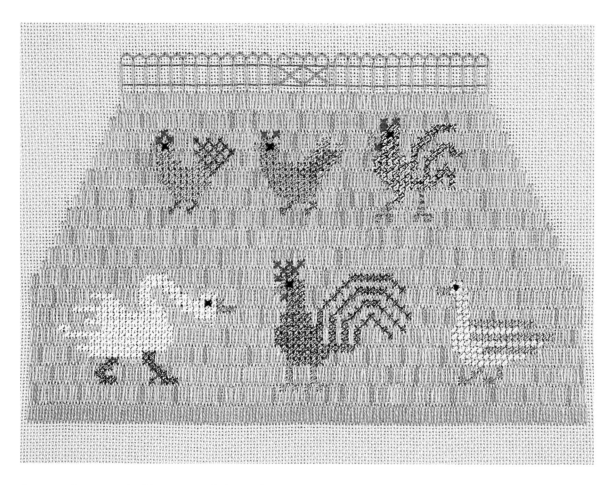

An area of grass worked in a range of blues, yellows and greens, makes an interesting and attractive background for a variety of domestic fowl, and in particular creates a very effective setting for the distinctive outlines of the swan motif.

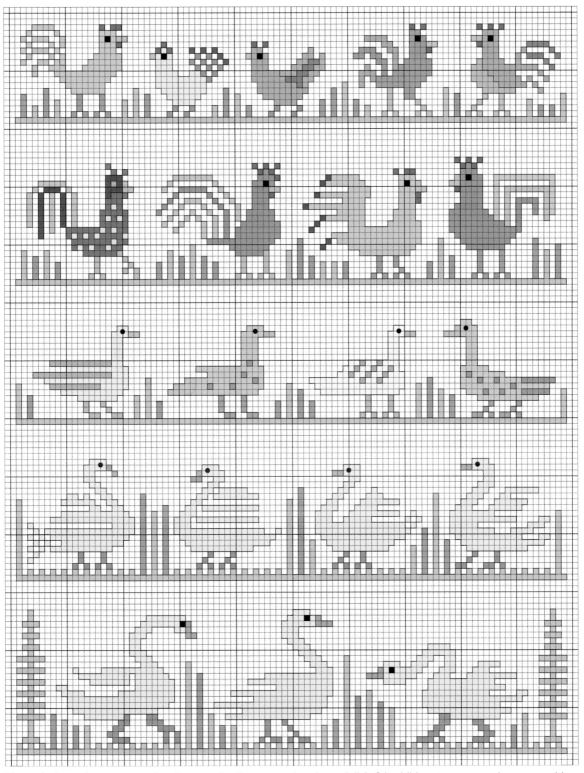

Hens, ducks and geese are often kept as family pets, and make a delightful addition to any sampler composition. In the past domestic fowl were associated with wealth and prosperity and some of the cockerel motifs that featured in earlier embroideries, could possibly have represented a particular prized specimen.

CHAPTER SIX
border patterns

The enthusiasm and passion for the embroidered flower was evident in almost every aspect of fashion and textiles in 17th century England, and this astonishing array of decorative needlework, was to provide the ideal inspiration for young girls beginning to learn a range of embroidery skills. The huge interest in plants and garden design meant that there were already several publications on the subject, and this was soon followed with books aimed specifically at the embroiderer, including a collection of stylised patterns depicting a variety of favourite garden flowers such as the rose, carnation, honeysuckle, lily and pansy. A series of rather formal designs containing stylised flower and leaf patterns, were to become a standard format for the perfectly stitched rows of decorative floral motifs that characterise the band sampler. The designs were transferred onto the fabric by a means of pricking out the pattern with a needle and then dusting the holes with charcoal powder, which left a clear outline for the embroiderer to follow. The whole design was then embroidered in double running-stitch, before larger areas of the composition were re-worked in a variety of stitch techniques, and occasionally metallic threads and beads were also added. Usually each row of patterns was embroidered in a different style, and whereas in one row, stems and trailing tendrils might be worked in stem-stitch, with outlined flowers and leaves filled in with satin-stitch and tent-stitch, another band might include a combination of cross-stitch and running-stitch techniques to describe the flower forms. Intricate white-work techniques were also practised and detailed black-work patterns were embroidered with delicate threads and precise stitches.

By the middle of the 18th century, the range of stitch techniques in general use had decreased considerably and the new interest in the pictorial sampler, together with the growing availability of cross-stitch patterns, meant that this simple and distinctive stylised stitch was to become the main technique associated with sampler embroidery, throughout the following two centuries and beyond. The shape of the sampler also began to change, and as it became wider in order to more easily accommodate the pictorial compositions, the bands of decorative floral motifs were placed around the edge of the design to form an attractive and appealing border pattern. The rigid and angular appearance of the formal designs from the previous century, were replaced with more realistic flower motifs arranged in flowing repeat patterns, with undulating stems and small leaf forms. A whole new range of floral patterns were adapted and developed from the original collection of stylised designs, with endless variations on the carnation, honeysuckle and strawberry motifs, which were to become the most popular and versatile as cross-stitch patterns, whilst other flowers such as the pansy, iris and rose gradually lost favour.

Another style of decorative floral border, based on freestyle embroidery techniques was also gaining in popularity alongside the cross-stitch patterns, and many embroiderers included both styles of work in the same sampler composition. This imaginative and creative form of needlework that combined decorative stylised flower motifs, with winding stems and waving leaves, was originally inspired by the free flowing, naturalistic designs imported from the Far East, which had also influenced the elaborate flower and plant motifs used to decorate household furnishings, and was generally referred to as crewelwork. The simple straight stitch techniques used in this style of embroidery, were ideally suited to creating a more expressive and individual interpretation of the plant forms, and motifs for carnations, tulips and roses, together with a whole variety of smaller flowers, were initially drawn freehand onto the fabric before being transformed into exquisite pieces of needlework.

Decorative border patterns in a whole range of styles and designs have been copied, adapted and altered in so many ways and with numerous variations over the course of time. However, the most popular types of flower motifs have always remained the carnation, rose, tulip and honeysuckle.

Several designs based on the acorn motif appear in many of the earliest pattern books, and variations on a stylised border pattern including the acorn with oak leaf, were very common throughout the seventeenth century. Further designs, for rows of simple leaf forms featured in later samplers.

Narrow bands of small repeat patterns were often included as a way of dividing the elaborate floral designs in early samplers, and as the pictorial composition evolved, they were also used as a means of separating lines of text, including alphabets and verse, from areas of figurative motifs.

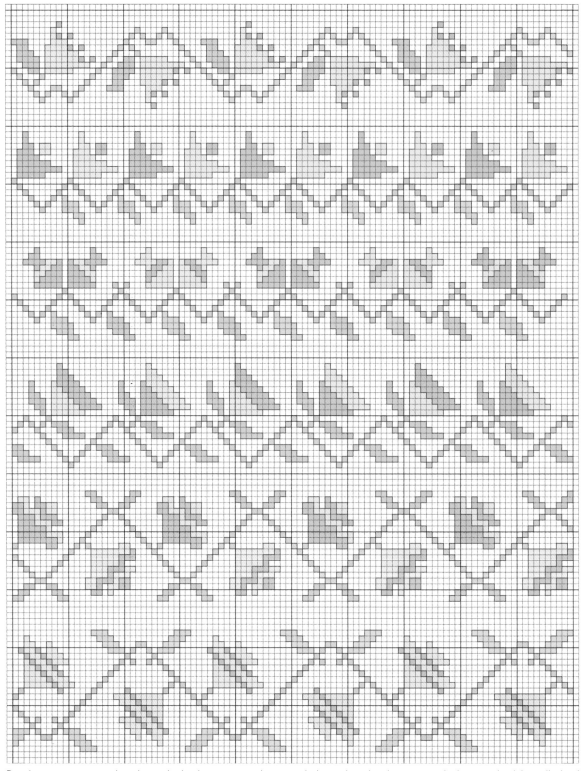

Border patterns can be deceptively time consuming to stitch, and a simple repeat design worked in a limited palette, can make a very effective frame to a composition, whereas more detailed designs could be included as a decorative band of pattern across the top or base of the sampler.

The overall appearance of a basic repeat pattern can be completely altered by using two or three different colour schemes for the flower motifs. The alternating colours convey a sense of movement in the design, and can give added interest to even the most simple border pattern.

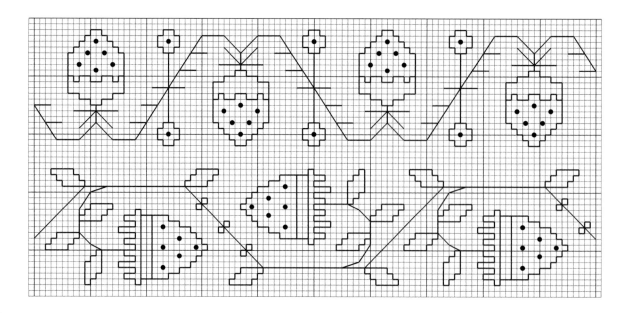

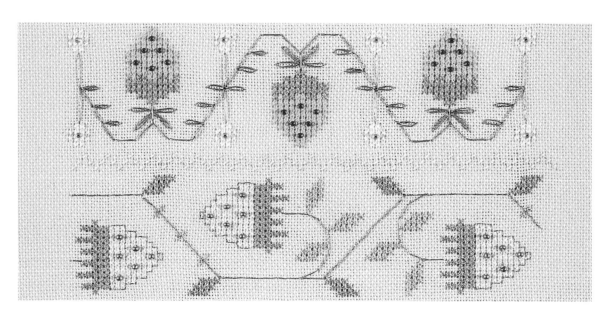

Threads: Anchor, DMC (skeins), Madeira no.40 (reel) Number of strands indicated in brackets.

STRAWBERRY (TOP DESIGN)
Light Pink – DMC 3609(1) + Madeira 1116(1)
Dark pink – Anchor 86(1) + Madeira 1117(1)
White Flower – Madeira 1222(3)
Stems – Madeira 1169(1) + Madeira 52(1)
– Back-stitch
Leaves – Madeira 1301(1) + Madeira 52(1)
– Lazy-daisy

STRAWBERRY (LOWER DESIGN)
White – Madeira 1222(2)
Pink – Anchor 86(1) + Madeira 1117(1)
Pink outline – Madeira 13(1)
Green – Madeira 1169(1) + Madeira 1301(1)
Beads Pink metallic size 15
Stems – Madeira 1169(1) – Back-stitch
Re-work stems – Madeira 52(1) Whip-stitch
Leaves dark – Madeira 1169 (1) + Madeira 1301(1)
Leaves light – Madeira 1169(1) + Madeira 1070(1)

The strawberry motif is one of the oldest and most popular patterns in existence, and has continued to feature in samplers throughout each century. Early examples often depict the fruit and flowers arranged in a plant form, but later border patterns were to become rather plain and uninspiring.

PINKS AND CARNATIONS

Carnations, pinks and picotees are all varieties of the same plant form, which has been inspiring artists for thousands of years, and many of the stylised patterns that became popular during the 17th century, may have been directly influenced by the designs on the ceramics and textiles that originated from Persia and the Near East. The attractive appearance and ornamental qualities of the flower are ideally suited to interpretation in needlework, and have become a favourite motif for the embroiderer, providing a wide range of possibilities for cross-stitch patterns. The fringed edges of the petals and the fan shaped arrangement of the open flower, has inspired endless permutations and variations of this most versatile of floral motifs.

This elaborate and most unusual carnation border, was originally inspired by a design in a band sampler worked by Ann Upton, and dated 1725, in the collection of the City of Bristol Museum and Art Gallery. The dynamic appearance of the design is created by the deep angles of the chevron patterns that represents the stems, together with the large stylised flower forms, and both these areas are further enhanced with an additional decoration of various small beads. The patterns and colour schemes for these designs feature on page 109.

The carnation was widely cultivated in England during the sixteenth century, when it was more commonly known as the gilliflower, due to its pungent scent. An early variety named Daintie Lady, was to inspire a number of designs, with its unusual colouring of red one side, and white the other.

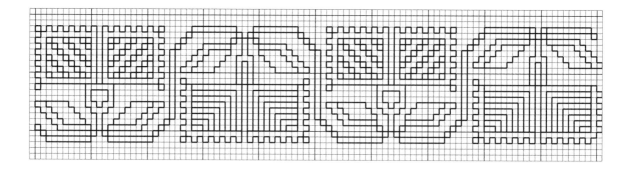

The highly stylised, squared format of this carnation motif reflects the type of patterns that were very popular during the eighteenth century. The compact arrangement of the motifs, together with the simple outlines and rich colours of the flowers, all combine to create a very bold and lively design.

CARNATION
Threads: Anchor, DMC (skeins), Madeira no.40 (reel) Number of strands indicated in brackets.

Pink – Anchor 98(1) + Madeira 13(1)
Red – DMC 3328(1) + Madeira 13(1)
White – Madeira 1222(1) + Madeira 1082(1)
Green dark – DMC 502(1) + Madeira 1360(1)
Green light – DMC 3819(1) + Madeira 1169(1)

The patterns and colour schemes for many of the stylised floral motifs are based on the characteristic markings of the various plants. Carnations include striped and flecked varieties with colours radiating from the centre, and the Picotee has colour round the outer edges of the petals.

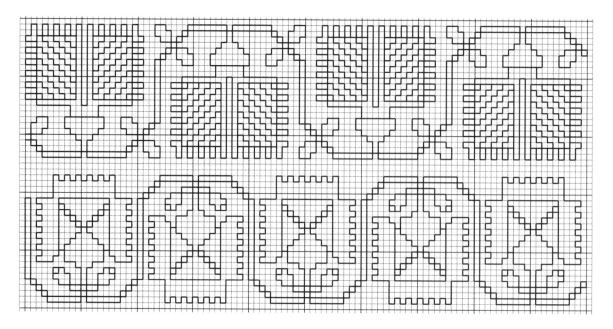

CARNATION

Threads: DMC (skeins), Madeira no.40 (reel) Number of strands indicated in brackets.

White – Madeira 1222(3)
Blue – Madeira 1360(2) + Madeira 301(1)
Yellow – DMC 729(1) + Madeira 1070(1)
Brown – DMC 435(1) + Madeira 1192 (1)

The enduring popularity of the carnation motif continued throughout the nineteenth century, and an attractive range of border designs worked in a combination of blues and ochre colours, made an interesting and eye-catching alternative to the usual choice of crimson and pink shades.

CARNATION

Threads: DMC (skeins), Madeira no.40 (reel) Number of strands indicated in brackets.

White – Madeira 1222(3)
Yellow – DMC 729(1) + Madeira 1070(1)
Brown – DMC 680(1) + Madeira 1192(1)
Blue – Madeira 1160(1) + Madeira 1360(1) + Madeira 301(1)

Motifs for a more naturalistic style of flower became popular during the nineteenth century, and a light and airy impression was created as the arcaded border patterns became wider and more spacious, occasionally including a group of flowers, with one large centre flower and two smaller buds.

TULIP

Threads: Anchor and DMC (skeins), Madeira
no.40 (reel)
Number of strands indicated in brackets.

Orange – Anchor 326(1) + Madeira 28(1)
Yellow – Madeira 1070(1) + Madeira 1025(1)

Brown – DMC 680(1) + Madeira 1065(1)
White – Madeira 1082(1) + Madeira 1222(1)
Lime Green - DMC 3819(1) + Madeira 1169(1)
Blue Green – DMC 502(1) + Madeira 1360(1)

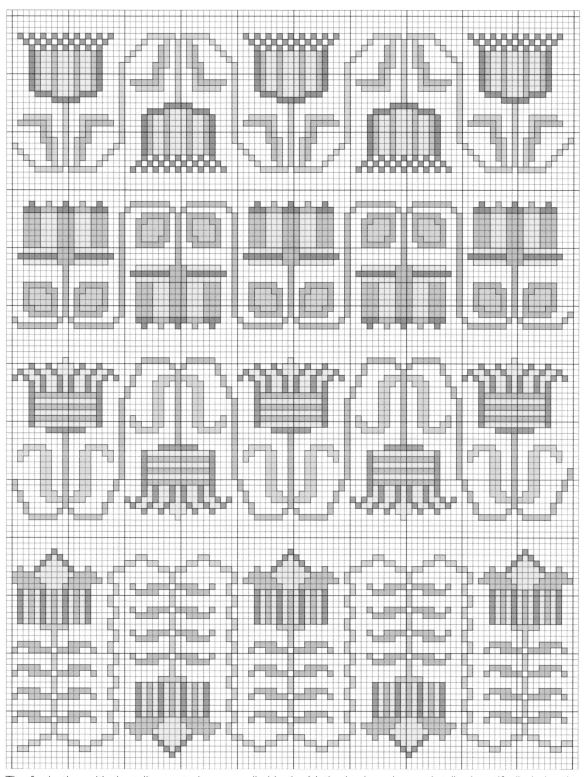

The fascination with the tulip was to be unequalled in the Netherlands, and several stylised motifs displaying the distinctive sculptural forms, feature in seventeenth century Dutch samplers. A number of these designs were later developed as repeat border patterns in English embroideries.

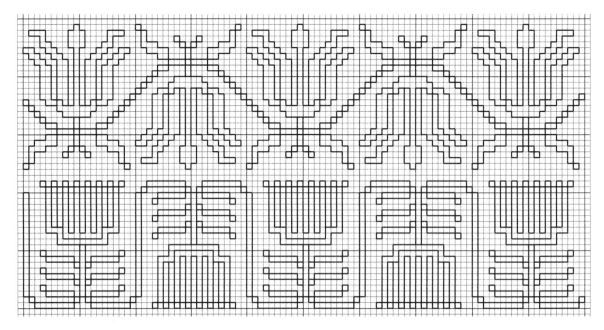

TULIP

Threads: Anchor and DMC (skeins), Madeira
no.40 (reel)
Number of strands indicated in brackets.

Light Pink – DMC 316(1) + Madeira 1080(1)
Orange – Anchor 316(1) + Madeira 28(1)
White – Madeira 1222(1) + Madeira 1082(1)

Stem: Green – Anchor 261(1) + Madeira 1169(1)
Leaves: Green – DMC 503(1) + Madeira 1360(1)
Pink - Anchor 87(1) + Madeira 13(1)

The tulip was first cultivated in England during the sixteenth century, and the elegant and shapely flower forms soon attracted much interest. It has since continued to feature as a favourite choice of border pattern, and a number of designs resemble the more open and feathery varieties of the plant.

HONEY SUCKLE

Threads: DMC (skeins), and Madeira no.40 (reel) Number of strands indicated in brackets.

Pink – Madeira 1309(2) + Madeira 13 (1)
Brown – DMC 976(1) + Madeira 28(1)
Beige/Gold – DMC 612(1) + Madeira 24(1)
White – Madeira 1222(2)

The delicate form of the honeysuckle made a very attractive subject for a number of naturalistically styled floral motifs, and was immensely popular as a border pattern throughout the eighteenth and nineteenth centuries, where it was usually portrayed in a range of pastel colour schemes.

The sweet scented honeysuckle or trailing woodbine, as it was commonly known, was a favourite flower of the seventeenth century embroiderer, and a number of very elaborate stylised patterns for a large flower motif, frequently appear in the band samplers from that period.

The Tudor Rose was closely associated with Elizabeth I, and the popularity of the stylised flower patterns continued to feature in samplers throughout the seventeenth century, alongside more complex designs that depicted the rose together with other smaller flower and leaf motifs.

CHAPTER SEVEN
floral arrangements

The subject of flowering plants featured in almost every aspect of Elizabethan life, and many of the designs and ideas related to the fashions, and needlework of the period, were all based on the theme of flowers. A growing interest and fascination with gardening and horticulture, meant that the humble posies, nosegays and sprigs of flowers that were routinely displayed in the 16th century household, were gradually joined by large elaborate arrangements, that combined familiar garden flowers such as roses, pinks and honeysuckle, with more unusual and ornate varieties of lilies, tulips and carnations. The sight of so many flower-filled vases, urns, tubs and baskets was a constant source of inspiration for the embroiderer, and the passion for needlework was so great that almost every publication on the subject of flowers, gardening and also herbals, was directed at the needlewoman. Illustrations for magnificent floral arrangements portraying large urns full of cascading flowers, together with stylised designs for single flowers, were all copied and adapted for further use in embroidery, and designs depicting a small sprig of flowers became a favourite subject for the embroidered motifs used in applied work, and generally referred to as slips. Many of the spot samplers from the 17th century feature examples of these attractive, naturalistic motifs, which were often cut out and re-stitched to cushions and furnishings. Band samplers from the same period include more formal motifs, with the flowers and leaves attached to winding stems and arranged in the form of a repeat pattern, and although some of the designs appear to suggest a display of flowers, they were not usually arranged in containers.

The stylised cross-stitch designs that were already in use in northern Europe, only occasionally appeared on English samplers in the 17th century and it was not until the following century, that motifs for a whole range of floral displays, were included in the pictorial compositions that were becoming increasingly popular. Stylised versions of tulips, carnations, roses and lilies were amongst the numerous designs for multi-flowering plants displayed in urns and vases, together with decorative arrangements in pretty baskets and motifs for single flowers sitting in little pots, all of which seemed to fill every spare space on the embroidery. Besides the patterns for large decorative flowerheads, a number of motifs depicted smaller flower forms that appeared as small circles, squares or bell shapes, which were arranged in the style of a growing plant, and often resembled a range of garden flowers such as foxgloves, hollyhocks, cornflowers, marigolds and daisies. Another series of patterns that most probably originated from the Netherlands, included many variations for a stylised motif depicting a pyramid shaped display of fruit in a bowl or basket. The decorative arrangement of the rounded fruits together with the angular patterns of the leaves, made a very attractive and colourful design, and was to become one of the most familiar and enduring sampler motifs.

The interest in combining freestyle embroidery techniques with cross-stitch patterns, meant that the two different styles of needlework were often featured in the same piece of embroidery. A very popular sampler composition that lasted throughout the 18th and 19th centuries, comprised of an elaborate floral arrangement depicting naturalistic flowers and leaves, embroidered in various freestyle techniques, which was surrounded by a verse and decorative border worked in cross-stitch. This particular format was often used to portray the numerous family record samplers, that were a feature of many American needlework schools. However, amongst some of the most imaginative embroideries that included freestyle techniques, were the compositions from the New England counties, that combined a dark background fabric with delicate leaf and flower forms all stitched in a variety of pastel coloured silks.

The contrasting styles of these attractive floral arrangements have been inspired by two samplers in the collection of the Victoria and Albert Museum. The highly stylised formal design is based on Mary Wakeling's sampler, 1744, and the more naturalistic composition has been adapted from Mary Ann Cook's sampler, 1812.

FLOWER ARRANGEMENT

The decorative flower forms in this design are based on an early 17th century pattern that features in numerous band samplers of the period, although it was to gradually disappear by the middle of the following century. There are many variations and individual interpretations of the original pattern, with each one seeming to have a different colour scheme, ranging from pastel shades, to bright reds and greens, and sombre browns and blues. The stems are often entwined with a decorative knot and the radiating flowers are occasionally surrounded by small birds. The stylised carnations are also depicted in various styles and techniques, with the flowers usually outlined in cross-stitch and the centres filled in with spots and flecks worked in seed stitch together with rows of double running stitch to create a striped pattern, and in other examples the flower forms are covered in satin-stitch to create a richly textured surface with a dense area of colour.

The original composition for this popular pattern has been adapted to form an arrangement of flowers displayed in a low trough, and the pink and blue colour scheme was inspired by a most unusual and extremely attractive example of the design, that features in a sampler by Katherine Carter, c.1670, in the collection of Witney Antiques. The pattern and colour scheme for this design features on page 110.

The larger more elaborate versions of this attractive motif, provided an ideal opportunity to create a very colourful and individual design. Occasionally a variety of fruits, such as pineapples, melons, cherries, grapes and even little strawberry plants were also added to the display.

FREE-STYLE EMBROIDERY TECHNIQUES

Compositions including a combination of cross-stitch and free-style embroidery techniques were particularly common during the 18th and early 19th centuries, and a decorative floral display of graceful arching stems, supporting a range of stylised flower forms was to feature as a central motif in many samplers. Designs were probably copied or adapted from the huge array of illustrations on the subject of flora, and initially a simple outline of the pattern would be drawn onto the fabric and used as a basic guide for the embroiderer to follow, working with simple running-stitch and back-stitch techniques. The flowers and leaves were then filled in with a series of short straight stitches, applied in several layers and arranged in the direction of the outlined form. Although this method of working can appear rather complex, it is in fact one of the easiest and most enjoyable of techniques, and the ability to alter and change the shade or intensity of a colour as the work is progressing, encourages a more creative and individual approach.

The pattern for this floral arrangement has been adapted to suit an evenweave fabric, with the design first outlined in back-stitch following a counted thread graph. The pattern and colour scheme for the design features on page 111.

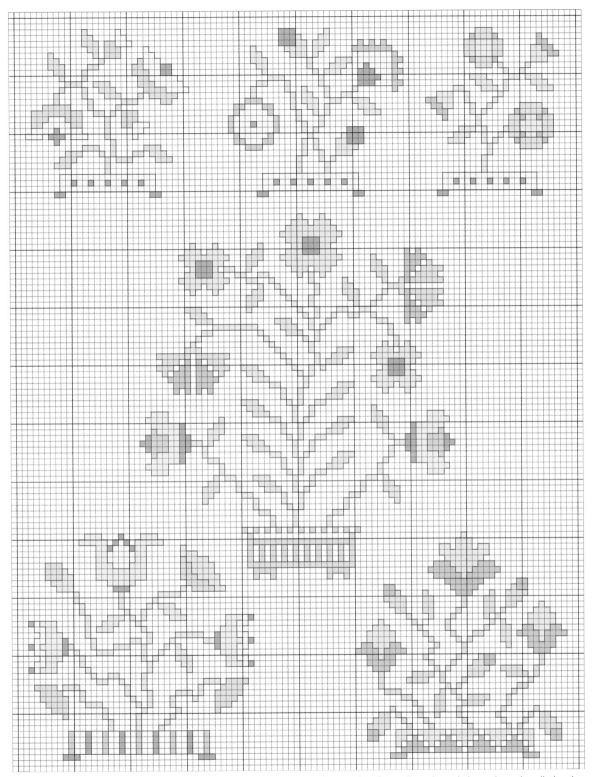

The arbitrary arrangement and the naturalistic style of these decorative flowering plants is based on the distinctive floral patterns that originated from the Ackworth School. The delicate appearance of the sinuous stems, are further complimented by the soft pastel colours of the flowers.

THE CREWELWORK STYLE.

The type of embroidery that is generally referred to as crewelwork encompasses many different styles and approaches, ranging from the flamboyant flower and leaf patterns that adorned curtains, bed-hangings and coverlets, to smaller pictorial scenes depicting stylised plants and trees surrounded by animals and birds, which featured on cushions, fire-screens and needlework pictures. The naturalistic style, of the delicate floral patterns that began to appear in sampler compositions during the 18th century, was directly influenced by the decorative painted designs for multi-flowering plants that featured on the Indian chintzes, which were flooding into both England and America at that time. Border patterns and floral arrangements now became a confusion of tumbling flower forms attached to winding stems, with a mixture of exaggerated and familiar garden flowers, all depicted in this most expressive of embroidery techniques.

The natural flowing forms of this multi-flowering plant includes a range of imaginary and stylised flowers, which have been embroidered with a variety of metallic and lustre threads to create a number of contrasting textural surfaces.

The various patterns for flowering plants that appear to be growing from a base at the ground, may have been a continuation of the type of natural plant motif that featured in earlier band samplers, and the idea of placing flowers in a container was possibly the influence of Dutch patterns.

The urns, tubs, vases and baskets that featured in many of the flower arrangements, were considered an equally important part of the design, presenting an opportunity for individual choice, and the huge range of styles and varying colour schemes make a delightful addition to any composition.

The pretty basket of flowers at the top of the page has been inspired by Mary Bates' sampler dated 1788, in the collection of the Embroiderers' Guild, and the lower design is adapted from Kitty Neve's most unusual composition dated 1818, in the collection of the Royal Pavilion & Museums, Brighton & Hove.

The traditional pictorial sampler features numerous patterns for stylised designs of flowers, displayed in decorative urns and vases. The simple format of the stem and leaf patterns, enables the different styles and sizes of the flower-heads to be interchanged with one another quite easily.

Various patterns for a large sunflower motif appear in several early German samplers, and a number of small scenes depicting rows of flowers and leafy plants growing amongst an area of grass, are featured in a sixteenth-century German sampler in the Victoria and Albert Museum collection.

appendix 1: graphs

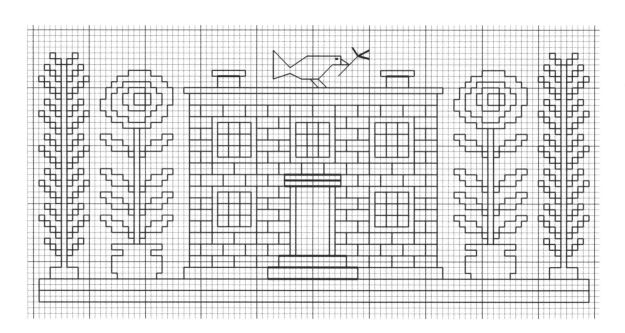

GEORGIAN HOUSE – CROSS-STITCH AND BACK-STITCH

The house is first worked in Cross-stitch and then the white lines for the bonding pattern are worked in Back-stitch.

Fabric: 28 Count Brittney – Light Mocha 309
Threads: Anchor and DMC (skeins), Madeira no.40 (reel) Number of strands indicated in brackets.

Walls
Brickwork – DMC 316(1) + DMC 224(1)
White lines – Anchor 300(1)

Windows
Frames – DMC 746(2)
Panes – DMC 647(1) + DMC 932(1)
Glazing bars – DMC 746(1)

Roof & base of House
Light brown – DMC 612(2)
Dark brown line – DMC 640(2)

Door – DMC 612(1) + DMC 640(1)
Knocker – DMC 640(1) - Double stitch

Steps & Lintel – DMC 613 (2)
Single line details – DMC 640(1)

Flower
Dark pink – DMC 316(2)
Light pink – DMC 3727(2)
Centre pink – DMC 3722(2)
Yellow – DMC 783(1) + DMC 743(1)

Stem – DMC 3348(2)
Leaves – DMC 471(2)

Flower pot – DMC 932(1) + DMC 807(1)

Fir Tree
Stem – DMC 503(1) + DMC 932(1)
Dark leaves – DMC 502(2)
Light leaves – DMC 503(1) + DMC 3813(1)

Grass – Straight-stitch using alternating colours.
Top row – DMC 471(1) + DMC 3348(1)
Bottom row – DMC 503(1) + DMC 3813(1)

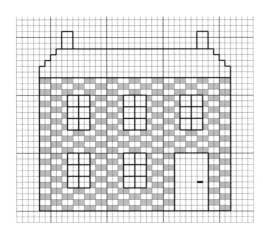

BRICK COTTAGE
Red Brick – DMC 3064(1) + DMC 612(1)
White Brick – DMC 746(1) + DMC 613(1)

Roof – DMC 926(1) + DMC 612(1)

Door – DMC 926(1) + DMC 613(1)

Window Panes – DMC 746(2)
Window Frames – DMC 926(1) – Back-stitch

Chimney – DMC 3064(1) + DMC 612(1)

WOODEN COTTAGE
White Walls – Madeira 1084(1) + Madeira 1222(1)

Brown outline of Building/Chimney &
Door Frame – DMC 3828(1) + Madeira 1126(1)

Narrow Brown lines &
Window Frames – Madeira 1126(1) – Petit-point

Window Panes - Anchor 920(1) + Madeira 1360(1)
Glazing Bars - Madeira 1126(1)

Door – DMC 729(1) + Madeira 1070(1)
Door knob - Madeira 1126(2)

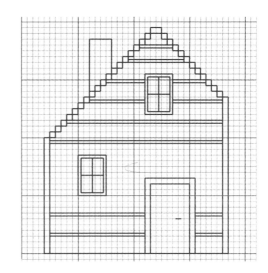

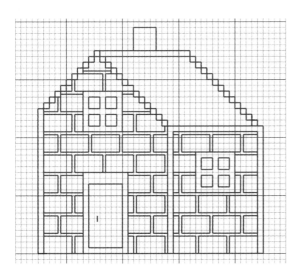

STONE COTTAGE
Stone-work – Madeira 1060(1) + Madeira 1055(1)
White lines – DMC 746(1) – Petit-point

Door Frame/ Window Frames/Chimney
& Brown outline - DMC 3828(1) + Madeira 1126(1)

Door – Anchor 215(1) + Madeira 1360(1)

Roof – DMC 3755(1) + DMC 642(1)

Window Panes – DMC 746(1) + Madeira 1222(1)

TUDOR FIGURES – CROSS-STITCH AND BACK-STITCH.

Fabric: 28 Count Brittney – Light Mocha 309

Threads: Anchor and DMC (skeins), Madeira no.40 (reel)Number of strands indicated in brackets.

Gold – Madeira 1070(1) + Madeira 24(1) + Madeira Gold 8(1)
White – Anchor 300(1) + Madeira 41(1)
Black – Madeira 251(2) + Madeira 70(1)
Pink – Anchor 63(1) + Madeira 18(1)
Blue – DMC 807(1) + Madeira 65(1)
Fans – Gold (as above) outline in Madeira 70(1)
Face/Hands – DMC 224(1) – Petit-point
Eyes – Madeira 70(1) – Seed-stitch
Mouth – Madeira 18(1) – Seed-stitch

Arch – square
Stems – Madeira 65(1)
Leaves/Green – Madeira 52(1) + Madeira 1169(1)
Leaves /Blue – Madeira 65(1) + Madeira 1169(1)

Flowers
Pink – Madeira 13(1) + Madeira 18(1)
White – Anchor 300(1) + Madeira 41(1)
Outline – Madeira 18(1)

Arch – round
Stems – Madeira 52(1)
Flowers – Madeira 13(1) + Madeira 18(1)
Flowers in Cross-stitch or Beadwork.
Grass – DMC 966(2) or DMC 3813(2)

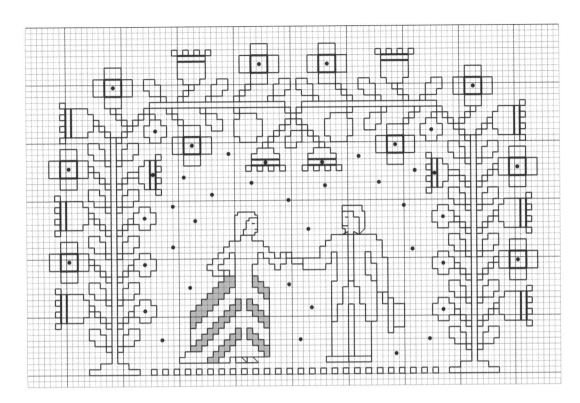

WEDDING SCENE – CROSS-STITCH AND BACK-STITCH

The Grey of the man's Jacket is re-worked with a half cross-stitch, facing to the right. The Dress is worked in cross-stitch, with the shaded area in a Gold colour. Pattern for Gold lines on Dress and position of beads – see small graph. Outline the whole Dress in Back-stitch.

Fabric: 28 Count Brittney - Light Mocha 309
Threads: Anchor and DMC (skeins), Madeira no.40 (reel) Number of strands indicated in brackets.

Groom's Jacket/Shoes & Brim of Hat – DMC 646(2)
Over-stitch Jacket – Madeira 1240(1) – single stitch / Shirt – Anchor 300(2)
Trousers & Hat – DMC 647(1) + Madeira 1060(1)
Hair Groom – DMC 612(1) – Petit-point
Hair Bride – DMC 611 (1) – Petit-point
Face/Hands (both) – Anchor 376(1) – Petit-point
Eyes (both) – Madeira 1240(1) Double seed-stitch
Mouth (both) – Madeira 1117(1) Single seed-stitch
Arch – DMC 612(1) + Madeira 24(1)
Gold lines – Madeira Gold 8 (1)
Beads – Pearl Seed beads – size 15

Dress – Cross-stitch
White – Anchor 300(1) + Madeira 300(2)
Gold (shaded area) – Anchor 300(1) + Madeira 24(1)
Lines on Dress – Madeira Gold 8 (1) – Back-stitch
Outline Dress – Madeira 251(1) – Back-stitch
Gold lines on Hair – Madeira Gold 8 (1)
Beads – Gold metallic & Pearl Seed bead – size 15
Shoes – Outline in Madeira 251(1), fill in Gold 8

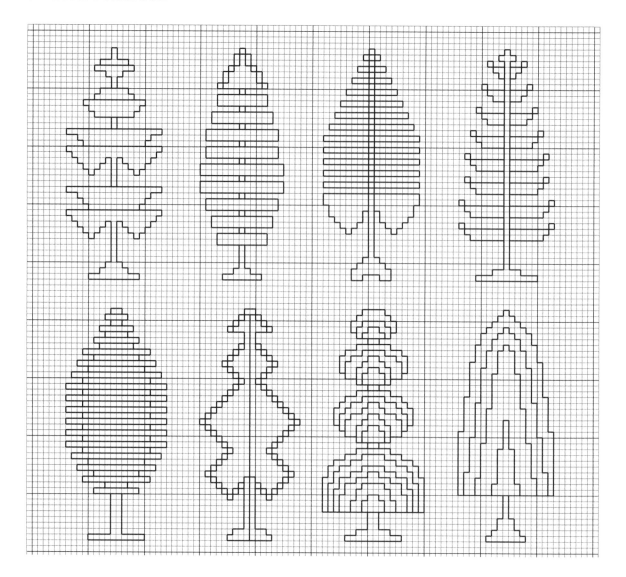

CONE SHAPED TREES – CROSS-STITCH.

These simple patterns could be interpreted in a number of different colour schemes, and interesting textural surfaces can be created with the addition of rayon or metallic threads to particular areas of the design.

Threads: DMC (skeins)-Number of strands indicated in brackets.
Green – DMC 471(1) + DMC 472(1)
Blue – DMC 503(1) + DMC 3813(1)
Yellow – DMC 834(1) + DMC 734(1)

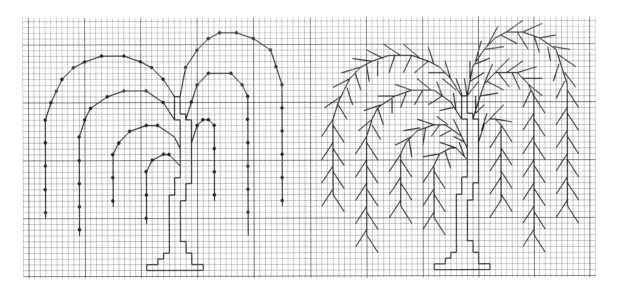

WILLOW TREE – BACK-STITCH AND LAZY-DAISY

Outline the trunk in Back-stitch and work a second colour inbetween the two lines. Work the branches in Back-stitch, length of stitches indicated by dots on graph. Leaves worked in Lazy-daisy, with alternating sets of colours.

Trunk outside lines – DMC 611(1)
Trunk inside line – DMC 612(1)
Branches – DMC 612(1)
Leaves (blue) – DMC 807(1) + DMC 471(1)
Leaves (green) – Anchor 215(1) + DMC 3348(1)

WILLOW TREE – BACK-STITCH, LAZY-DAISY AND CROSS-STITCH.

Work trunk in Cross-stitch and branches in Back-stitch, length of stitches indicated by dots on graph. Leaves worked in Lazy-daisy, with alternating sets of colours.

Trunk – DMC 611(1) + DMC 613(1)
Branches – DMC 612(1)
Leaves (blue) – DMC 807(1) + DMC 471(1)
Leaves (green) – Anchor 215(1) + DMC 3348(1)

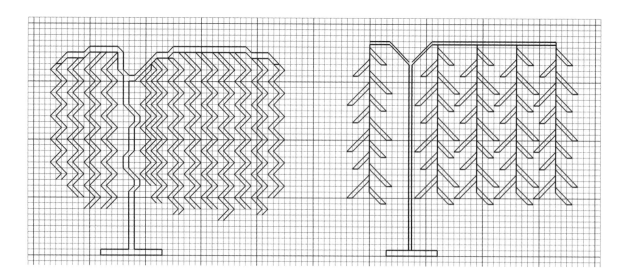

WILLOW TREE – ABOVE LEFT

Outline the Trunk in Back-stitch and work a second colour inbetween the two lines.

Trunk outside lines – DMC 734(1)
Trunk inside line – DMC 370(1)

Each branch is worked with three rows of back-stitch, see page 48

Green Branch
– Anchor 255(1) – Row 1& 2
– DMC 472(1) – Row 3

Blue Branch
– DMC 3816(1) – Row 1
– Anchor 875(1) – Row 2 & 3

WILLOW TREE – ABOVE RIGHT

Trunk and Branches – DMC 370(1) – Back-stitch

The leaves are outlined in Back-stitch and a further stitch placed in the centre. Alternate branches have different sets of colours for the leaves, see page 48

Leaves (set 1) – Anchor 875(1) and DMC 470(1)
Leaves (set 2) – DMC 471(1) and DMC 3816 (1)

CROSS-STICH WILLOW TREES

Designs on page 48

Willow Tree – left image
Trunk – DMC 612(1) + Madeira 1070(1)

Branches
Green – DMC 471(1) + DMC 472(1)
Blue – DMC 503(1) + DMC 3813(1)
Yellow – DMC 834(1) + DMC 734(1)

Willow Tree – Right image
Trunk – DMC 734(1) + Madeira 1055(1)
Branches – Anchor 875(1) - Back-stitch

Alternate branches have different sets of colours for the leaves, see page 48

Leaves (set 1)
– Blue – DMC 3816(1) + Anchor 875(1)
– Green – DMC 3819(1) + DMC 734(1)

Leaves (set 2)
– Blue – DMC 3766(1) + DMC 3816(1)
– Green – DMC 3819(1) + Anchor 255(1)

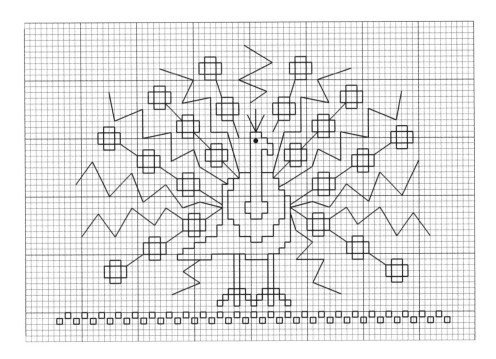

PEACOCK – CROSS-STITCH AND BACK-STITCH

Fabric: 28 Count Brittney – Light Mocha 309

Threads: DMC (skeins), Madeira no.40 (reel) Number of strands indicated in brackets.

Blue-Body/Head – DMC 807(1) + Madeira 52(1)

Gold-Body/Legs – Madeira 24(1) + Madeira Gold 8(1) + Madeira 1070(1)

Spots
Red – DMC 3805(1) + Madeira 18(1)
Silver – Madeira 41(1) + Madeira Alu (1) + Madeira 1071(1)

Brown - DMC 434(1) + Madeira 28(1)
Gold – Madeira 24(1) + Madeira Gold 8(1) + Madeira 1070(1)

Gold Lines – Madeira Gold 8 (2) – Back-stitch
Blue Lines – Madeira 65(2) – Back-stitch

Eye – DMC 3805(2) + Madeira 18(1) – French-knot
Crown – Madeira 18(2)

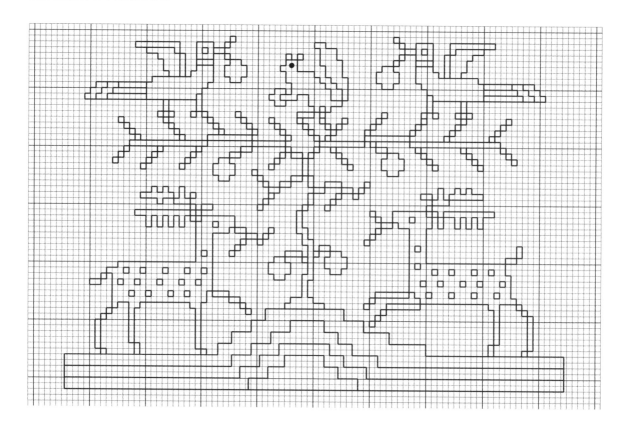

DEER – CROSS-STITCH AND BACK-STITCH

Fabric: 28 Count Brittney – Light Mocha 309
Threads: Anchor and DMC (skeins), Madeira no.40 (reel) Number of strands indicated in brackets.

Deer – DMC 435(1) + Madeira 1158(1) + Madeira 2210(1)
White spots – DMC 746(2)
Antlers – DMC 611(1) + Madeira 2210(1)
Eye – DMC 3371(2)

Tree
Trunk – DMC 612(1) + Madeira 2210(1)
Leaves – DMC 807(1) + Anchor 255(1)
Fruit – DMC 223(2)

Squirrel – DMC 435(1) + Madeira 2210(1)
Eye – DMC 3371(2)

Bird
Light Brown – DMC 612(1) + Madeira 1055(1)
Dark Brown – DMC 611(2)
Blue – DMC 807(1) + DMC 926(1)
Eye – DMC 3371(2)

The grass is worked in a diagonal straight stitch using sets of alternating colours.
Blue set – DMC 807(1) + DMC 581(1)
Green set – DMC 581(1) + Anchor 255(1)
Yellow set – DMC 3820(1) + DMC 3348(1)

CARNATION BORDER PATTERNS –
CROSS-STITCH AND BACK-STITCH.

Fabric: 28 Count Brittney – Light Mocha 309
Threads: Anchor and DMC (skeins), Madeira no.40 (reel) Number of strands indicated in brackets.

Top pattern
Green – DMC 3819(1) + Madeira 1169(1)
Dark Pink – Anchor 86(1) + Madeira 13(1)
Light Pink – Madeira 1116(3)
White – Madeira 1222(3)

Lower pattern
Outline the stems in Back-stitch, working over two diagonal stitches.

Re-work the stems in Whip-stitch.

Light Pink – Madeira 1116(2) + Madeira 13(1)
Dark Pink – Madeira 1117(2) + Madeira 13(1)
White – Madeira 1222(3)
Green Cross-stitch – Madeira 1169(1) + Madeira 52(1)
Green Back-stitch – Madeira 1169(1)
Green Whip-stitch – Madeira 52(1)

Beads – Green Pink foiled seed beads, size 15.
White pearl seed beads, size 15.

FLOWER ARRANGEMENT – CROSS-STITCH AND BACK-STITCH

Work flowers in Cross-stitch – Pink (shaded areas) and White in centres.

Re-work Blue lines in Back-stitch.

Fabric: 28 Count Brittney – Light Mocha 309
Threads: Anchor and DMC (skeins), Madeira no.40 (reel) Number of strands indicated in brackets.

Flowers
Pink – Anchor 86(1) + Madeira 1117(1)

White – Madeira 1222(3)
Blue line – Madeira 1094(1) + Madeira 33(1)

Leaves and Stems
Green – DMC 734(1) + Madeira 1169(1)
White – Madeira 1222(3)

Trough
Blue – DMC 932(1) + Madeira 1094(1)
White – Madeira 1222(3)
Blue line – Madeira 1094(1) + Madeira 33(1)

VASE OF FLOWERS – CROSS-STITCH AND STRAIGHT STITCHES

Leaves and flowers – Outline in back-stitch and fill in the areas with a series of small straight stitches using embroidery cottons, so as to almost cover the fabric (see graph detail). Then re-work with a rayon thread, following the direction of the stitches. Stems – follow graph line in back-stitch and then re-work with a whip-stitch, working over the surface stitches.

Fabric: 28 Count Brittney – Light Mocha 309
Threads: DMC (skeins), Madeira no.40 (reel)
Number of strands indicated in brackets.

Vase – Madeira 1222(2) – Cross-stitch
Blue spots – Madeira 1360(1) + Madeira 1047(1)
Outline – Madeira 1360(1) – Back-stitch
White lines across top and base – Madeira 1222(1)

Leaves – Outline – Madeira 1169(1) – Back-stitch
Fill in with straight stitches – DMC 3819(1)
Re-work with straight stitches – Madeira 1047(1)

Stems – Madeira 1169(1) – Back-stitch
Re-work with – Madeira 1047(1) – Whip-stitch

Green base of flowers, outline in Madeira 1169(1) & Fill in with small straight stitches using colours above.

Carnations – Outline in Madeira 1309(1)
Fill in with small straight stitches – DMC 3823(1)
Re-work, to cover surface – Madeira 1222(1)

Pink Rose – Outline in Madeira 1309(1)
Fill in with small straight stitches – DMC 224(1)
Re-work, to cover surface – Madeira 1116(1)
Centre -Cross-stitch
White – DMC 3823 (1) + Madeira 1222(1)
Yellow – Madeira 1065(3)
Buds – Pink-Madeira 1169(1)
Buds – Yellow – Madeira 1025(1)

Tulips – Outline in Madeira 1025(1)
Fill in white areas – DMC 3823(1)
Re-work white with – Madeira 1222(1)
Fill in yellow areas – DMC 3046(1)
Outline edge of petals again – Madeira 1065(1)
Small yellow marks on tulip – Madeira 1065(2)
(See graph detail)

111

appendix 2: alphabets and text

The inclusion of alphabets, numerals and verse in the traditional sampler composition provided an opportunity for various styles of lettering to be incorporated in both a decorative and informative way, as part of the overall design. The ability to record family names, dates and actual places, and thereby personalise a pictorial image, is one of the main reasons for the popularity of this style of folk art. In general, the majority of early band samplers comprised of decorative floral patterns, but the use of text as part of an embroidery design, became standard practise as young girls were instructed to sign and date their needlework exercises. The regular uniformity of the cross-stitch technique made it an ideal method for interpreting the angular shapes of the letterforms, and the teaching of alphabets and numerals gradually became commonplace. Many samplers included long verses on a religious or moral theme, with an emphasis on virtue and obedience, although sometimes additional information such as the name of the school, the teacher or a particular building was also added, and has helped to provide an interesting piece of social history. However, embroidery was not only confined to the school-room, as needlework was very much a part of a woman's everyday life, and love messages, initialled love-tokens and even full length letters were occasionally stitched onto fabric. Making a record of the family register was also a favourite subject and in a number of samplers it became the central theme of the composition, with perhaps a border of flowers arranged around the text, or alternatively a large motif of a tree formed the main area of the design, with the family names and dates placed around the branches. Sometimes these samplers were kept folded away in a drawer, and added to by various members of the family, with each successive birth, death or marriage. With the renewed interest in sampler-making during the second half of the 20th century, the idea of making an embroidery specifically to celebrate a special occasion became very popular, with samplers to commemorate notable events such as births, christenings, weddings, and anniversaries and also the family group and home.

Planning the content, arrangement, and style of the lettering can be great fun and will add much interest to the finished work. Where you place the text in relation to the overall design, and the choice of a letterform that will best compliment the theme of the work, will all need careful thought and consideration. Firstly write out all the details you wish to include on a piece of paper and perhaps try making a number of different arrangements with the words. Then count up the space that is available in the embroidery, choose an alphabet style that you feel is appropriate, and chart out the letters on a sheet of graph paper, although at this stage you may have to make several adjustments to the spacing of the words and letters, in order for the text to fit neatly in the given area. There are many different styles of alphabets to choose from, and it is quite easy to alter the letterforms to suit a particular length by, either extending or reducing the width of an individual letter, adding tails and flourishes, or placing the words closer or further apart. The colours you select to illustrate the various pieces of text will also play an important part in the overall appearance of the embroidery, with light or dark tones placing a different emphasis on the words. I usually prefer to use fairly neutral colours for areas of cross-stitch text, and very small lettering in Back-stitch may need to be worked in a deeper shade, whereas a large decorative alphabet would provide many more options for creating different effects, with the addition of metallic threads and beadwork.

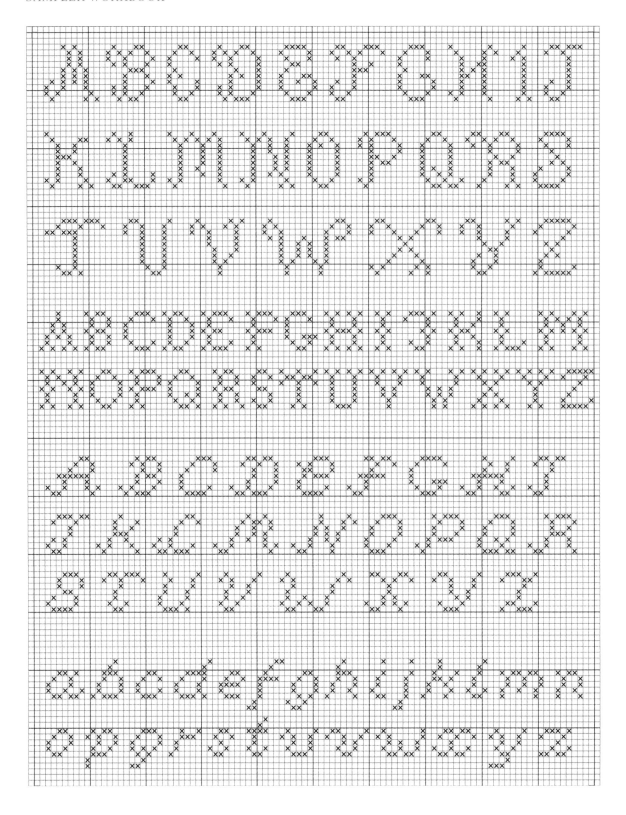

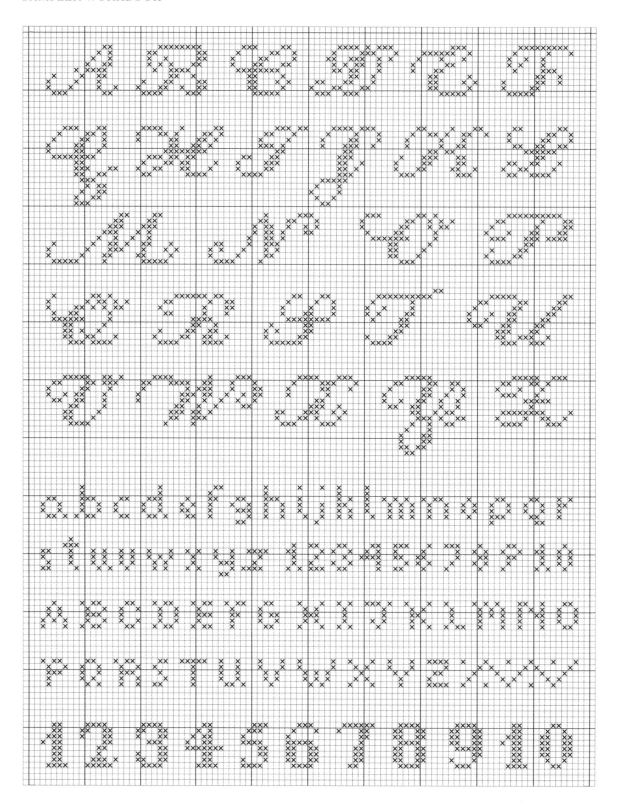

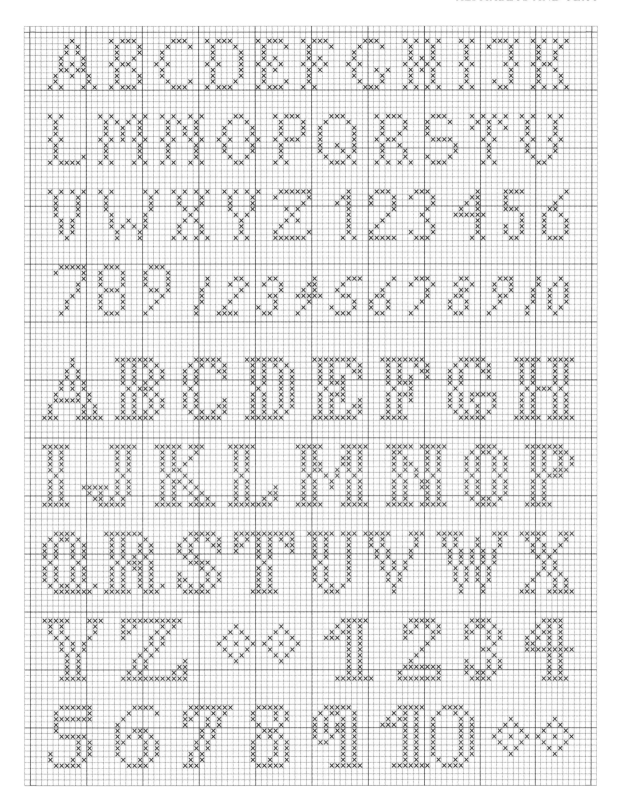

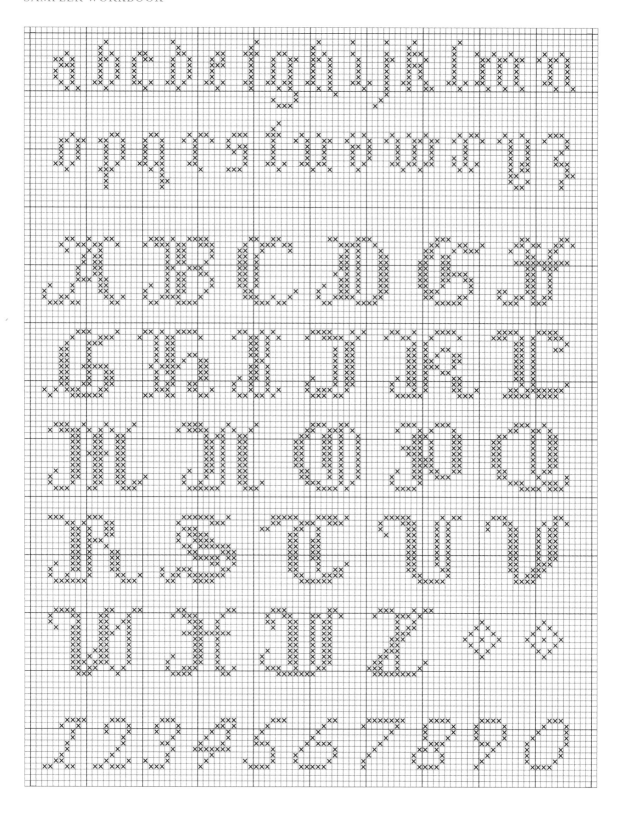

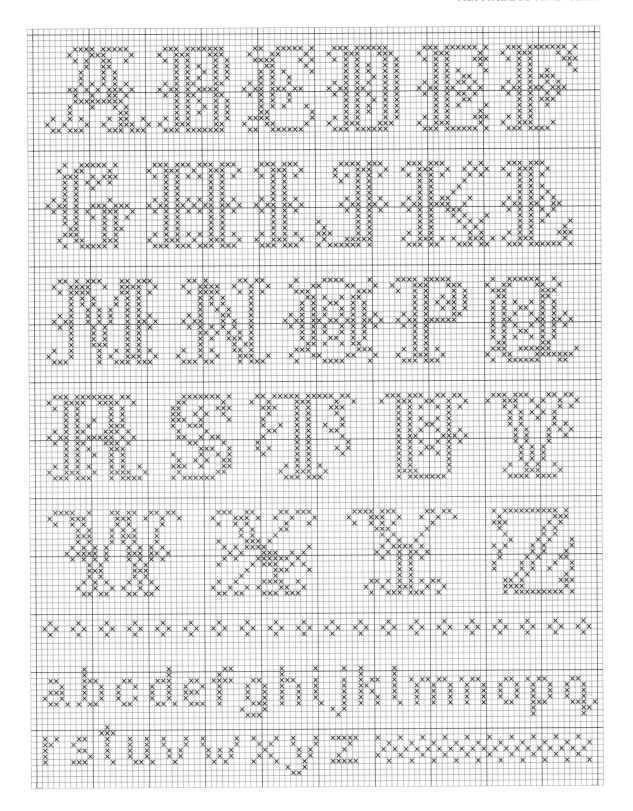

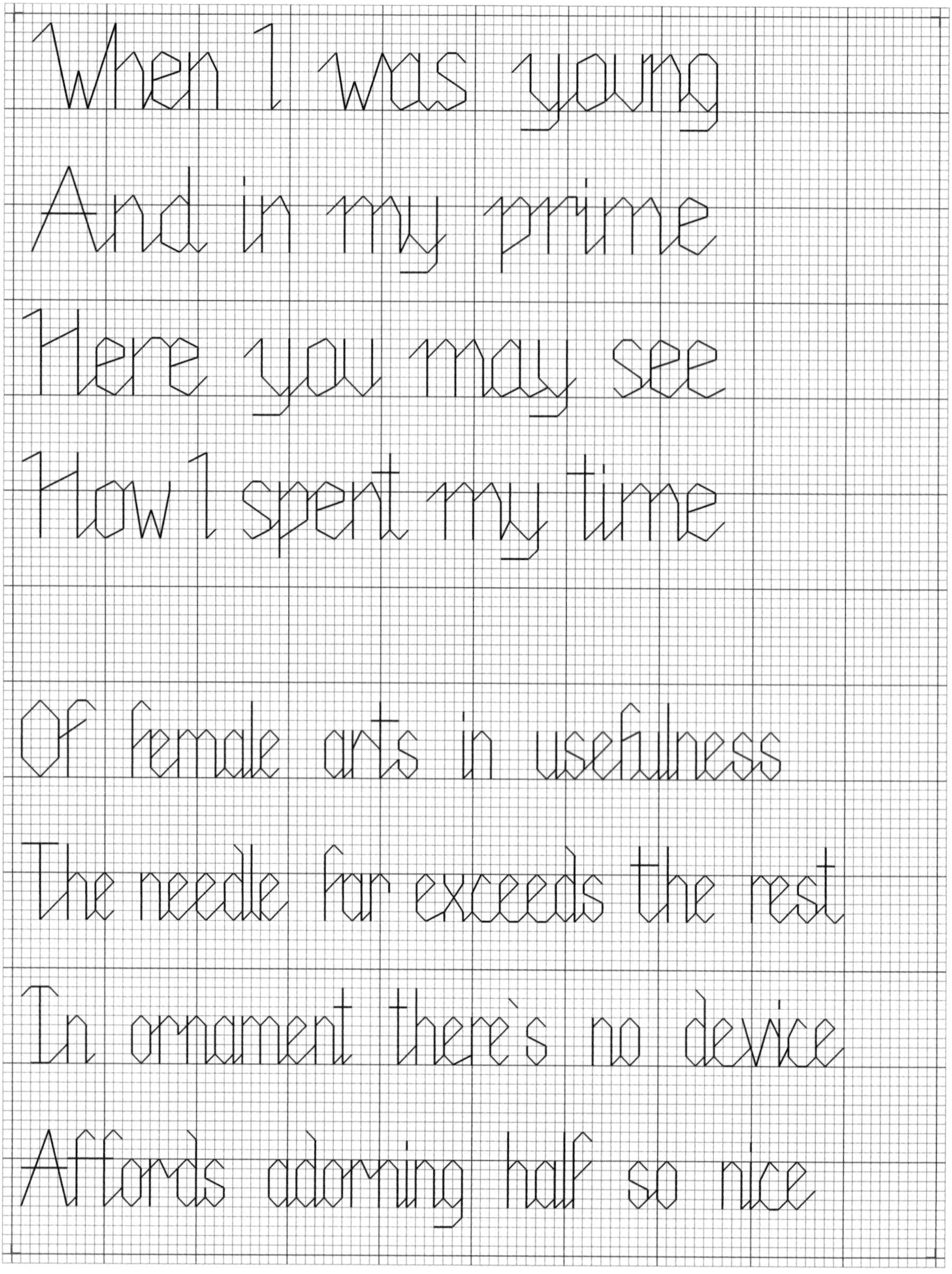

When 1 was young

And in my prime

Here you may see

How 1 spent my time

Of female arts in usefulness

The needle far exceeds the rest

In ornament there's no device

Affords adorning half so nice

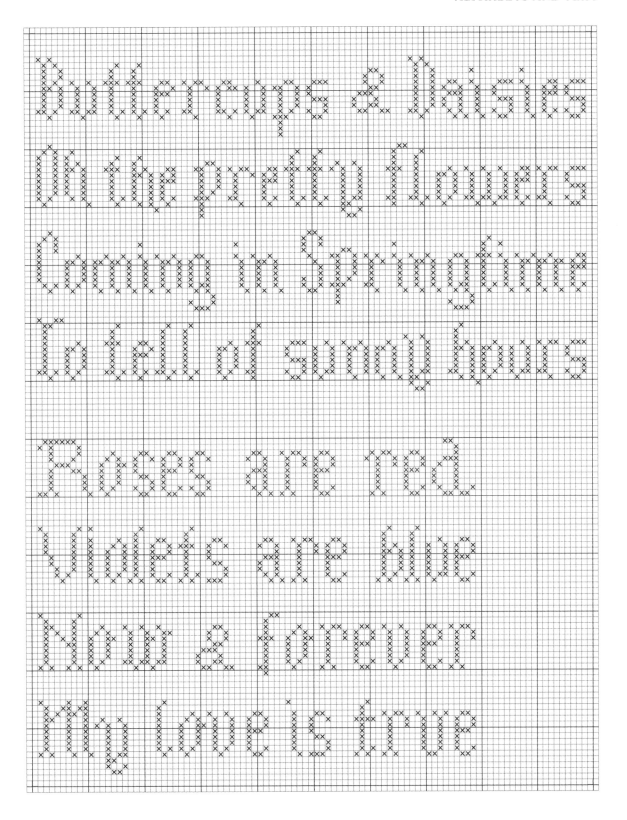

Buttercups & Daisies

In the pretty flowers

Coming in Springtime

To tell of sunny hours

Roses are red

Violets are blue

Now & forever

My love is true

glossary

Applied work. Embroidered motifs of flowers, birds, and animals worked on linen, which are then cut out from the background fabric and re-stitched to a heavier material such as velvet or satin, to form decorative design on cushions and garments.

Band samplers. A term used to describe a style of sampler that dates from the early 17th century, which included horizontal rows of floral patterns, alphabets and occasionally pictorial scenes, worked on a narrow length of linen.

Berlin Work. The brightly coloured embroideries were worked in wools on an open canvas and often included naturalistic shading on the patterns. By the middle if the 19th century, designs were being printed directly onto the canvas, and supplied with the appropriate coloured wools.

Blackwork. A popular form of needlework, that was used to decorate various items of clothing, during the Tudor period. Detailed and intricate patterns were outlined in black threads using a double-running stitch, and the technique appears frequently in many band samplers.

Boxer Figure. A small male figure depicted in a walking position with head turned sideways, and carrying a flower, branch or fruit in one hand. In early examples the figures were naked and usually worked in a double running stitch, but gradually various forms of clothing were added to the motif.

Canvaswork A form of pictorial needlework, that became popular during the 16th century, and was mainly used in the production of domestic furnishings. Cross-stitch and tent-stitch techniques were worked on fine linen canvas, using wool and silk threads.

Crewelwork. Although the decorative designs were originally worked in lightly twisted woollen yarns applied to a heavy linen twill, and used for bed curtains and coverlets, the free-style embroidery techniques were later adapted to the smaller scale of the sampler embroidery.

Prick and pounce. This is a term used to describe a popular, traditional method for transferring designs onto fabric. A fine muslin bag was filled with powdered charcoal or chalk, and then patted gently over the pin-pricks that had been carefully made, following a paper pattern. Once the design was removed, the lines of small dots were painted over with a fine wet brush

Slips. Individual motifs depicting small plants, or floral cuttings from a plant, which were usually worked in a very fine tent-stitch or petit-point, and intended to be cut out from the original background and applied to another fabric.

Spot sampler. An embroidery depicting a series of motifs that were usually scattered in a random arrangement across the fabric, which was particularly popular at the beginning of the 17th century, and besides various floral and geometric patterns many examples also reflected the fashionable interest in exotic species of animals, birds, insects and plants.

Tent stitch. A technique used mainly in needle-point embroidery, where the entire background fabric is covered in a series of stitches, slanting in the same direction. On furnishing textiles various worsted wools were worked onto coarse linen, but the technique was also applied to very fine needlework, using silk threads and light-weight muslins.

Whitework. A style of embroidery that was very popular during the 17th century, and consisted of floral and geometric designs worked in white threads on linen, which were often arranged in the form of a band sampler. Many of the patterns were influenced by lacework techniques, and would include examples of cutwork, drawnwork, and hollie-point.

reference notes

BURRELL COLLECTION, GLASGOW MUSEUMS

Page 38 Frances Cheyney – dated 1663. Ref.31.20.
Page 38 Jane Turner – dated 1668. Ref. 31.8.
Page 60 English spot sampler – c 1625-1630. Ref. 31.1.

CITY OF BRISTOL MUSEUM

Page 72 Ann Upton – dated 1725.Ref N3913

DORSET COUNTY MUSEUM.

Page 58 English spot sampler – dated 1630.

EMBROIDERERS' GUILD, HAMPTON COURT PALACE.

Page 97 Mary Bates – dated 1788. Ref.EG3

FITZWILLIAM MUSEUM, CAMBRIDGE.

Page 14 English Band Sampler – c1660. Ref.T.31-1928
Page 28 Anne Lawle – dated 1655 or 1665. Ref.T.15-1928

GLOUCESTER FOLK MUSEUM.

Page 27 Mary Carpenter, Glocester – dated 1788.

GOODHART COLLECTION, MONTACUTE HOUSE, NATIONAL TRUST

Page 28 English Sampler – dated 1778. Ref.MON/G/082
Page 60 English Band Sampler – mid 17th century. Ref. MON/G/021
Page 34 English Band sampler – mid 17th century. Ref. MON/G/028

ROYAL PAVILLION & MUSEUMS, BRIGHTON & HOVE

Page 97 Kitty Neve – dated 1818. Ref.CT 003781

VICTORIA AND ALBERT MUSEUM

Page 14 Margret Mason – dated 1660. Ref. T.182-1987
Page 14 Elizabeth Cridland – dated 1752. Ref. 288-1886
Page 28 Elizabeth Short – dated 1661. Ref. T.131-1961
Page 30 Long cushion cover – c.1600. Ref. T.79-1946
Page 38 and 99 German Sampler - first half 16 century. Ref. T.114-1956
Page 38 and 58 Jane Bostocke – dated 1598. Ref. T.190-1960
Page 60 English sampler - first quarter 17 century. Ref. 9047-1863
Page 89 Mary Wakeling - dated 1742. Ref. 394-1878
Page 89 Mary Ann Cook - dated 1813. Ref. T.100-1939

WITNEY ANTIQUES.

Page 14 Elizabeth Sexton – dated 1660
Page 28 English Sampler, initialled EI. – dated 1656
Page 39 Ann Davis – dated 1808
Page 51 Sarah Gilbank – dated 1766
Page 56 German Sampler, initialled HSH – dated 1789
Page 56 German Sampler, initialled IDG – dated 1758
Page 60 Mary Cock – dated 1812
Page 90 Katherine Carter – c.1670

places to visit

MUSEUMS IN THE UNITED KINGDOM

The American Museum in Britain, Bath.
Tel. 01225 460503

City of Bristol Museum and Art Gallery.
Tel. 01272 223571

Fitzwilliam Museum, Cambridge.
Tel. 01223 332900

Glasgow Museum
The Burrell Collection.
Tel. 0141 287 2550

National Trust Montacute House.
The Goodhart Collection.
Tel. 01932 823289

Parham House, Sussex.
Tel. 01903 742021

Victoria & Albert Museum, London.
Tel. 0207 9422000

Whitby Museum, Yorkshire.
Tel. 01947 602908

Whitney Antiques, Oxon.
Tel. 01993 703902

MUSEUMS IN EUROPE

German Sampler Museum, Celle.
Tel. +49 (0) 51141 382626
The collection of Elfi & Hans-Joachim Connerman

Netherlands Open Air Museum.
Tel. +31 (0)26-3576111

MUSEUMS IN AMERICA

American Folk Art Museum, New York
Tel. 212-265-1040

Museum of Fine Arts, Boston
Tel. 617-267-9300

The Metropolitian Museum of Art, New York.
Tel. 212-979-5500

The Sampler Gallery, Old Saybrook.
Tel. 860-388-6809
The collection of Stephen & Carol Huber

suppliers and manfacturers

SUPPLIERS

Barn Yarns (Ripon) Ltd.
Canal Wharf
Bondgate Green
Ripon
North Yorks HG4 1AQ
Tel. 01765 690069

The Bead Merchant
P.O. Box 5025
Coggeshall
Essex CO6 1HW
Tel. 01787 221955

Willow Fabrics
95 Town Lane
Mobberley
Knutsford
Cheshire WA16 7HH
Tel. 01565 872225

Wye Needlecraft
2 Royal Oak Place
Matlock Street
Bakewell
Derbyshire DE45 1HD
Tel. 01629 815198

MANUFACTURERS

Coats Crafts UK
Lingfield House
Lingfield Point
McMullen Road
Darlington
County Durham DL1 1YJ
Tel. 01325 394394

DMC Creative World
First Floor Compass Building
Seldspar Close
Warrens Park
Enderby
Leicestershire LE19 4SD
Tel. 01162 754000

Madeira UK Ltd
12 Hallikeld Close
Barber Business Park
Melmerby
Ripon
North Yorkshire HG4 5GZ
Tel. 01765 640003

bibliography

Bromiley Phelan, Dorothy. Hanson, Eva-lotta. Holdsworth, Jaqueline: *The Goodhart Samplers*, Needleprint (2008)

Brown, Clare & Wearden, Jennifer: *Samplers from the Victoria and Albert Museum*, V & A Publications (2003)

Colby, Averil: *Samplers, Yesterday and Today*, B T Batsford, Ltd., London (1964)

Don, Sarah: *Traditional Embroidered Animals*, David & Charles, (1990)

Edmonds, Mary Jaene: *Samplers and Samplermakers* (An American Schoolgirl Art1700-1850), Rizzoli International Publications, Inc. (1991)

Ehrman, Edwina: *The Judith Hayle Samplers*, Needleprint, Guildford (2001)

Fawdry, Marguerite and Brown, Deborah: *The Book of Samplers*, Lutterworth Press (1980)

Gierl, Irmgard: *The Sampler Book*, A&C Black London (1987)

Huber, Stephen & Carol: *Samplers how to compare & value*, Octopus Publishing Group (2002)

Humphrey, Carol: *Samplers*, Fitzwilliam Museum, Cambridge University Press (1997)

Jarrett, Joy and Scott, Rebecca: *Samplers*, Shire Books (2009)

Jarrett, Joy & Stephen, Scott, Rebecca: Various sampler exhibition catalogues, Witney Antiques (see: www.witneyantiques.com)

King, Donald & Levey, Santina: *The Victoria & Albert Museum's Textile Collection Embroidery in Britain from 1200 to 1750*, Victoria and Albert Museum (1993)

Krueger, Glee: *A Gallery of American Samplers The Theodore H.Kapnek Collection*, Bonanza Books, New York (1984)

Meulenbelt-Nieuwberg, Alberta: *Embroidery Motifs From Dutch Samplers*, Batsford (1974)

Parker, Rozsika: *The Subversive Stitch*, The Women's Press (1984)

Pearson, Lu Emily: *Elizabethans at Home*, Stamford University Press (1957)

Quinton, Rebecca: *Patterns Of Childhood Samplers from Glasgow Museum*, The Herbert Press an imprint of A & C Black (2005)

Ring, Betty: *American Samplers and Pictorial Needlework, 1650-1850 Girlhood Embroidery* (vols 1&2), Alfred A. Knopf, inc. (1993)

Roach, Audrey: *Secrets of a Sampler*, Country Life, May 2003.

Sebba, Anne: *Samplers: Five Centuries of a Gentle Craft*, Thames & Hudson (1979)

Shorelyker, R: *A Schole-house for the Needle*, RJL Smith & Associates (1998)

Stevens, Christine: *Samplers From the Welsh Folk Museum Collection*, National Museum of Wales (1987)

Symonds, Mary and Preece, Louisa: *Needlework Through the Ages*, Hodder and Stoughton (1928)

Walton, Karin-M: *Samplers In The City Of Bristol Museum & Art Gallery*, City of Bristol Museum & art gallery (1983)

Wilder Lane, Rose: *Womans Day Book of American Needlework*, B. T. Batsford Ltd London, Simon and Schuster New York (1963)

index